THE BURDEN

THE BURDEN

AFRICAN AMERICANS AND THE ENDURING IMPACT OF SLAVERY

ROCHELLE RILEY

WITH A FOREWORD BY
NIKOLE HANNAH-JONES

FEATURING ESSAYISTS

Mark Auslander, Kevin B. Blackistone, Herb Boyd, A'Lelia Bundles,
Charlene A. Carruthers, Betty DeRamus, Carolyn Edgar, Patrice Gaines,
Aisha Hinds, Aku Kadogo, T'Keyah Crystal Keymáh, Torrance G. Latham,
Paula Williams Madison, Julianne Malveaux, Tonya M. Matthews,
Vann R. Newkirk II, Leonard Pitts Jr., Tim Reid, Michael Simanga,
Michelle Singletary, DeWayne Wickham, Benét J. Wilson,
and Tamara Winfrey-Harris

Wayne State University Press | Detroit

ISBN 978-0-8143-4514-6 (jacketed cloth);
ISBN 978-0-8143-4515-3 (ebook)
Library of Congress Cataloging Number: 2017952072

Published with support from the Arthur L. Johnson Fund for African American Studies.

Wayne State University Press
Leonard N. Simons Building
4809 Woodward Avenue
Detroit, Michigan 48201-1309

Visit us online at wsupress.wayne.edu

To all those who came before . . .
the great-grandparents, grandparents, parents, and families,
who, like mine, raised excellence from oppression

CONTENTS

FOREWORD
Nikole Hannah-Jones

One can learn about a nation as much by what it remembers as by what it forgets.

The ruling class carefully constructs a narrative that becomes the national memory, a glorification of a people and a land. And in America, the heart of that narrative has always been our exceptionalism, our birthright as a nation born of the quest for freedom, a nation that has existed as a beacon for oppressed, liberty-seeking people everywhere.

And then there's us. The dark race that casts the dark shadow on this magnificent narrative.

How do we deal with the fact that our nation's greatness was built, quite literally, on the backs of the enslaved? That our decision to deprive an entire race of people of the fundamental rights laid out so clearly in the Declaration of Independence predates the founding of our country by nearly 160 years? That after Thomas Jefferson penned this Declaration, it would take 192 years for, legally at least, the beatific assertion "All men are created equal" to include those whose ancestors were stolen from the African continent?

How do we rectify these contradictions?

By rendering them to obscurity.

We pretend that slavery and the belief systems that sustained it were a mutation rather than our nature. That it was an unprofitable and paternalistic system of labor practiced by a small number of backward Southerners, not the economic engine that propelled this nation into one of the most prosperous the world has ever seen.

Slavery is embedded in the very DNA of this great and conflicted country. It took the deadliest war in American history to force its demise, and then we simply replaced this system with another form of racial apartheid. This new system forced generations of black Americans, like my grandparents and my father, born on a sharecropping farm in Greenwood, Miss., into a form of quasi-slavery that the Supreme Court condoned when it wrote in 1857 that the black man had no rights that the white man need respect.

Entire frameworks were constructed to enforce this system of racial caste that allowed my ancestors to be stripped of their rights, their labor, their families, their bodies, themselves. Black people were barred from moving to some states, from remaining in certain towns after the sun went down, from living on certain streets, from buying homes in white communities, from attending school with white children, from swimming with their white neighbors, from checking out books at the libraries that their tax dollars helped pay for, from parking in whites-only parking spaces, from working jobs reserved for white people. Nothing, and I mean nothing, was untouched by the racial caste system that justified slavery.

I was born in 1976, just eight years after the violent throes of riots that inflamed more than one hundred U.S. cities following the assassination of Dr. Martin Luther King Jr. Had I been born just a few years before, I would have taken my first breaths as a citizen of a country where it was legal to deny me housing for no other reason than I was descended from the enslaved.

Yet we learn almost nothing about this. Slavery is presented as an aberration in a still-striving nation, the years of Jim Crow that followed often summed up in our school history texts as an unfortunate blip that quickly ended after some black college students got ketchup and mustard dumped on their heads at a Southern lunch counter.

We choose to forget that slavery was a national scourge—that Northern states also allowed slavery, that the entire nation profited from it. Congress, after passing the 13th Amendment, realized that it was not enough to outlaw the institution of slavery, and so it passed civil rights laws in the 1860s to eliminate the "badges" of slavery as well. A hundred years later, in ruling against a white community that prohibited black residents from moving in, the Supreme Court ruled that the 13th Amendment had "clothed" Congress with "power to pass all laws necessary and proper for abolishing all badges and incidents of slavery in the United States," and that it empowered Congress "to eradicate the last vestiges and incidents of a society half slave and half free."

The badge of slavery wasn't our skin. It was the conditions created to demean, degrade, exploit, and control those with our skin. We have never rid ourselves of those badges, not in the 1860s, not in the 1960s, not now. We remain a nation of full citizens and part citizens. And our original sin remains the thing for which we—the people the sin was visited upon—can never be forgiven: our very presence here reminds this great nation of all that we are not.

And now, despite the fact that black Americans remain at the bottom of every indicator of well-being in this country—from wealth, to poverty, to health, to infant mortality, to graduation rates, to incarceration—we want to pretend that this current reality has nothing to do with the racial caste system that was legally enforced for most of the time the United States of America has existed.

The election of Barack Obama was the exception, the election of Donald Trump the correction. And this uncomfortable truth drives the urgency for this book. We must face this history, our heritage, if we do not want to be lassoed to the past.

James Baldwin said, "Not everything that is faced can be changed; but nothing can be changed until it is faced."

This book, with its unflinching truths and its damning prose, forces us to face the enduring legacy of slavery, and to face it now. This book will not fix what needs to be fixed, but it is a necessary step forward, a demand that the journey begin.

THE BURDEN

INTRODUCTION

Rochelle Riley

I will not shut up about slavery.

It is not a distant memory that African Americans should get over, relegate to dust, like the millions of Africans who did not survive it.

It is not something that began and ended like a beating or a trial.

It was instituted and embraced to build a country. Then it evolved, and hundreds of years later remains ingrained in the way we live, whether we are those watching from an uncomfortable, sometimes guilty perch or listing on the edge of despair and irrelevance every day.

Slavery still matters, and for those who live with the burden of continued enslavement, the continuing assaults disguised as painful memories, the heinous misconceptions, the rampant criminalization, or the deliberate efforts to diminish our talent, it still hurts. It still affects our ability to achieve, to live in total freedom.

Americans, black and white, have spent centuries recovering from a system of legal brutality that yielded to illegal brutality that yielded to illegal discrimination that yielded to covert discrimination that sometimes is not hidden at all. Much of white America has spent centuries racesplaining: mocking the idea that racism exists or demanding evidence of it or expressing sorrow about it while doing little or nothing to end it.

Enslavement did not end. It just changed addresses. It slowly, over a century and a half, moved into the bastions of government and the headquarters of corporations and the benches of the nation's courtrooms and the desks of the nation's classrooms, and to our newspapers and television stations. Yes, as with most things, some of it is the media's fault.

What America refuses to accept is what Dr. W. E. B. Du Bois predicted, that the color line would be the problem of the 20th century. There would have been no way for him to know that the system that corroded America then would continue to be the problem of the 21st century now, and that so many African Americans would be fooled into believing that slavery had ended.

African Americans were enslaved longer than we have been free, and since emancipation, have spent a century and a half fighting to make that freedom real. It is a battle that led to a 1954 court decision requiring fair education, a 1965 act of Congress granting voting rights, and a 1968 act banning housing discrimination—and we're still fighting to enforce *those* laws. We do that while battling a justice system that imprisons black people at more than 5 times the rate of whites, according to The Sentencing Project, a Washington, DC-based nonprofit that promotes criminal justice. That's not freedom. That's the clinging vine of slavery by another name still shackling a race.

This project had been brewing in my head for years, but the pot boiled over three years ago when columnist Jack Kelly of the *Pittsburgh Post-Gazette* wrote this blasphemy: "Slavery was horrible, but no black American living today has suffered from it. Most are better off than if their ancestors had remained in Africa." Columnists don't usually respond to one another. We respect one another's opinions, no matter how misguided. But I couldn't resist and asked in a Facebook post: "Which African countries has he visited to feed his presumption? And what studies did he cite to show that nearly three centuries of forced labor and outlawed education had no impact on descendants who couldn't bequeath capital and lifestyle and wealth the way slave-owners could? And if I hear one more ill-informed commentator criticize the disintegration of the black family as if slavery didn't disintegrate black families—separating mothers from daughters, husbands from wives—my scream will be heard for three states."

This collection of narratives, essays, rants, and heartbreaking reveals is a response to the false idea that slavery wasn't so bad, that we should just get over it. I searched for voices to offer contextual affirmation of what I've felt, what I've seen, what I've reported in a 37-year journalism career.

In this book are voices whose songs are sung in different keys, accompanied by different instruments—all sharing in their own way how they feel about an industrial system that continues to guide America.

These writers offer their thoughts on carrying the burden, passing that burden to their children and living with the damage that affects how America sees us and how we see one another.

Slavery continues to color our journey—darkly.

Always has. Always will.

Until we put the burden down.

THE BURDEN
Rochelle Riley

The scene is seared into my memory. Red, just paroled from Shawshank Prison, works as a bag boy at a local grocer. He quickly packs a sack for a customer, then raises his hand to catch the manager's attention.

"Restroom break, boss?"

His white supervisor calls him over.

"You don't need to ask me every time you need to take a piss. Just go, understand?"

Red nods quickly, acquiescently. He goes to the men's room. As he stands over the urinal, his words, in voiceover, hang in the air:

"Forty years I been asking permission to piss. I can't squeeze a drop without say-so."

That is what prison did to a grown man in a fictional film, *The Shawshank Redemption*.

That is what being enslaved did to a people.

There are thousands and thousands of examples in written history that detail the physical brutality of slavery. But what America must pay more attention to is the emotional brutality that boils down to a single, post-slavery word that has been as much a part of our living history as our flag:

Permission.

Permission to speak.

Permission to vote.

Permission to work in jobs that allow us to use all of our talents.

Permission to drink from community water fountains.

Permission to dine at public lunch counters.

Permission to sit anywhere on public buses that our tax dollars fund.

Permission to provide our children with educations equal to those of their white peers.

Permission to embrace the freedom the Emancipation Proclamation lied about.

Permission to run for the presidency of the United States of America.

We—African Americans in the United States—have spent a century and a half seeking permission, hiding our lights under bushels, accepting less than we deserve because we've been trained to believe we don't deserve more.

It is time to put that burden down.

Slavery is not a relic to be buried, but a wound that has not been allowed to heal. You cannot heal what you do not treat. You cannot treat what you do not see as a problem. And America continues to look the other way, to ask African Americans to turn the other cheek, to suppress our joy, to downplay our achievements, to accept that we are supposed to go only as far as we are allowed.

For more than two decades as a newspaper columnist, every time I write a positive, life-affirming column about the success of a black person, I expect the email, letter, or phone call. And it always comes.

"Why do you write so much about black people?" he, she, they ask.

And I always answer:

"Well, sir (or ma'am), the first thing you must remember is: I'm black. The second is: I am keenly aware of what I write, and after counting the number of columns I have written specifically about black people or issues, I have determined that it's about 35 percent of all of my columns. So, two things are true: I need to write more about black issues, and I need to write more about black people."

"But," I typically continue, "here's my question: Why are you so bothered that I write about black people?"

The answers are as varied as the levels of prejudice. One said, "We can never move on if you keep pointing out differences." Another said, "You're too talented to do that."

Still another said, "Just stop."

Just stop.

Apparently, he had not given me permission.

Why talk about slavery? Why talk about race? Why not move on?

The answer is simple: There is no moving on when it is so hard for African Americans to move.

The Civil War wasn't just between the states; it was between the past and future, between black and white.

It is the longest domestic war in American history. And it is not over. It just devolved into skirmishes—legal, brutal, emotional, sometimes behind-closed-doors battles. It became the looser enslavement we endure now. The sad thing is we believe that we are free. We believed the hype. We believed the dream.

But every day, we are reminded of that past—whether by politicians trying to diminish voting rights or by having to Americasplain black history to the masses.

When America celebrated the 70th anniversary of Jackie Robinson's desegregrating modern Major League Baseball, the quote that circulated on Twitter wasn't about his joy at joining a white team. It was this one, from his 1972 autobiography, *I Never Had It Made*:

There I was, the black grandson of a slave, the son of a black share-cropper, part of a historic occasion, a symbolic hero to my people. The air was sparkling. The sunlight was warm. The band struck up the national anthem. The flag billowed in the wind. It should have been a glorious moment for me as the stirring words of the national anthem poured from the stands. Perhaps, it was, but then again, perhaps, the anthem could be called the theme song for a drama called The Noble Experiment. *Today, as I look back on that opening game of my first world series, I must tell you that it was Mr. Rickey's drama and that I was only a principal actor. As I write this twenty years later, I cannot stand and sing the anthem. I cannot salute the flag; I know that I am a black man in a white world. In 1972, in 1947, at my birth in 1919, I know that I never had it made.*

African Americans have been moving targets, moving but not allowed to move too far, for a century and a half, confronted with racism, sometimes beneath the surface, sometimes in our faces, but all the time, anytime, even when we least expect it.

It was explained brilliantly in a scene from Shonda Rhimes's ABC television show *Grey's Anatomy*, when Maggie, a black doctor, tells a white colleague, Amelia, how it feels:

"Well it's not an issue . . . for you. And it's not all of a sudden. I mean, OK, it's not *Mississippi Burning* or anything, but it is all over. It's when people assume I'm a nurse, or when I go to get on an airplane with my first-class ticket, and they tell me that they're not boarding coach yet. It's like a low buzz in the background. And sometimes you don't even notice it, and sometimes it's loud and annoying, and sometimes it can get dangerous, and sometimes it is ridiculous—like right now."

For nearly 250 years, we could do nothing but suffer.

For more than 150 years since, under that low buzz that sometimes rises, we have been seeking permission to stop suffering.

We have been asking permission to seek joy from the very people whose ancestors enslaved ours and who need African Americans to be inferior to ensure their assumed racial superiority. Nazi leader Adolf Hitler's folly was that his hubris and hate were so public. So sure was he of his righteousness that he paraded his bigotry and efforts to create a superior race. He didn't realize he was going to hell until he killed himself in a bunker in April 1945—and maybe not even then.

Racists have existed for centuries. We tolerate them, endure them, watch the ebb and flow of their efforts, which have been made easier by our government, our education system, our elected leaders' cowardice. Through the years, we black Americans have watched our culture appropriated and desegregation attempted on the backs of our children. We watched the federal government explicitly participate in housing segregation.

In an interview with NPR's Terry Gross, Richard Rothstein, author of *The Color of Law*, detailed how the Federal Housing Administration ensured segregation by engaging in redlining—"refusing to insure mortgages in and near African American neighborhoods."

The F.H.A. subsidized builders creating subdivisions for whites —"with the requirement that none of the homes be sold to African Americans"—while African Americans were pushed into urban projects.

"The segregation of our metropolitan areas today leads . . . to stagnant inequality, because families are much less able to be upwardly mobile when they're living in segregated neighborhoods where opportunity is absent," Rothstein said. "If we want greater equality in this society, if we want a lowering of the hostility between police and young African American men, we need to take steps to desegregate."

That is easier said than done in a culture in which African Americans still are not treated equally by banks and segregation remains easy to maintain. As recently as April 2017, a federal judge allowed a predominantly white suburb in Birmingham, Ala., to secede from the predominantly black Jefferson County school district, according to a *Washington Post* report. District Judge Madeline Haikala admitted that racial motives "assail the dignity of black schoolchildren," and that the community of Gardendale "could not prove that their actions wouldn't hinder desegregation in Jefferson County." But she allowed it anyway, ruling that parents deserve local control over schools and adding that she was concerned for black students who had been made to feel unwelcome.

Right.

My awareness of the low buzz and the level of anger I felt at my own lost history, came in a conversation with my grandfather in 1988.

I am not quite sure of the exact place or exact date of my birth, but at any rate I suspect I must have been born somewhere and at some time.

—Booker T. Washington

I was a reporter at *The Washington Post*. I was visiting our family home in Tarboro, N.C., for the weekend, and I had finally decided to ask my grandfather about his past. We grew up learning to not ask, learning to not push too far. My grandfather, Bennie Pitt, was a man of few words, most of them gruff. But he was a good husband and father to his two daughters and his youngest daughter's three children, whom he and his wife, my grandmother, Lowney Hilliard Pitt, raised.

He was a frightening man to his grandchildren, my friends, and most of our neighbors, who all cowered a little in his presence. I often wondered whether his persona, built from years of gruffness, was a way to claim the power and respect he should have had just by being an American man but was denied because he was an African American man.

The stature he demanded was affirmed every day when I heard people address him on the street by his surname, sometimes by his full name: "Morning, Mr. Pitt!" "Hey, Mr. Bennie Pitt."

It was affirmed further by his refusing to call people by their given names. He called every man and boy "Charlie."

"Hey, Charlie!" he'd shout to Mr. Davis across the street, whose first name was Alexander. And all of them, every one, would answer, "Hey, Mr. Pitt!"

That sunny afternoon, as we sat on the porch of my growing up house, and I asked him about the ancestors, I could sense his impatience within minutes. We traveled back, generation by generation, from him to his father, Nathaniel, to his grandfather Ad, to his great-grandfather Bailum.

He always stopped at Bailum, either because that was as far as he knew or because that was as far as he dared go.

He gave me the name, but not the circumstances. He refused to talk much about growing up in the bend of the river, the Tar River, in eastern North Carolina.

But I was a reporter. I was undaunted.

I drove an hour and a half to Raleigh, our state capital, to review census records and birth and death certificates.

I found Bailum in death. But that whetted my appetite to know more. I wanted to find him in life. I finally did, in the property tax records of an Edgecombe County lawyer named Pitt. I found the death certificate of his wife, Jane, but could find no more. I resigned myself to knowing I'd never learn how tall she was, the color of her skin or the size of her smile.

Every discovery in my search for my family's history led to a heartache I can explain only by reminding people why it was such a big deal that the author Alex Haley searched for and found the roots of his own family tree in a village in Gambia, to know that there was a beginning somewhere.

I carry that quietly, a sack of hurt, a bundle of unsatisfied curiosity that never goes away. As I got older, I realized that I was looking for more than a beginning of my family. I was looking for an origin for the hatred, because the greatest burden I carried as a parent was knowing that I would have to give that burden to my daughter, that one day she'd be in a classroom with children who knew their grand-parents and great-grandparents and great-great-grandparents—and she never would.

I counted the days until that would happen by counting the days and weeks until someone would call that sweet-faced child "nigger."

She was five.

The little red-headed girl on the bus that carried them from their elementary school to day care will never know the damage she did.

My first thought was that it happened so much sooner than when it happened to me. My first time, years before, I was covering Richard Petty's birthday party at his sprawling estate in western North Carolina. A first-year reporter for the *Greensboro Daily News and Record*, I was the only black person among about five hundred people on the grounds of his farm, and my notebook—in those days, we carried notebooks—was my protection. I remember returning to the newsroom and mentioning what happened to our managing editor, Ned Kline, who called Petty and laid him low for what happened.

Two years later, I was working for *The Dallas Times Herald* in the cop shop of the Dallas Police Department headquarters. Every day, I walked past the spot where Jack Ruby shot Lee Harvey Oswald and wound my way into that little room shared by my newspaper and the *Dallas Morning News.*

Every day, we perused police reports searching for stories. A wonderfully gruff reporter who worked for the competition helped me determine what was worth my time. He told me to skip TNDs.

"What are those?" I asked.

"Typical nigger deals," he casually said. "You won't want those."

Speechless, I couldn't tell whether I was more stunned that he said it or that he didn't consider me one. He turned out to be a great help some evenings. And his editors never knew that he occasionally double-checked to make sure I was aware of the big stories. I always was, but I still marveled at his concern.

Imagine spending your life, and your child's, wondering not if you'd hear it, but when you'd hear it directed at your child.

It wasn't just the word; it was the expectation.

I came to loathe the word "minority" almost as much. When my daughter was in fourth grade at an advanced elementary school, she came home upset one afternoon. When I asked why, she said she made a 90 on her test, rather than 100.

"Well, let's see what happened," I said.

There were nine correctly spelled words and one blank.

She had missed "quiche."

"Honey. How did you miss that one?"

"I didn't know what that was."

"Yes, you do. It's the egg pie that we have at La Madeleine."

"Oh! Then she should have said egg pie." But my daughter added: "My teacher said it doesn't matter. I don't have to get the best grades because I'm a minority, and we'll always be OK."

Thank God we weren't on the freeway, or I might have caused an accident turning the car around in traffic. I chose to wait until the next morning to chat with her teacher, who I'm sure never, ever said that to a black child again. I became a room parent, at least for a few days, to make sure.

The constant reminder of the attempt to make African Americans inferior was never clearer to me than when I realized how little American children learn about African Americans.

One day, my dearest friend in Louisville, Joanna Gnau, went to pick my daughter up from school because I was tied up in news meetings. An hour later, she called me in tears to tell me she was on her way back.

My heart stopped.

"What's wrong? Is she all right? Did you have an accident?"

She explained that when she arrived at school, my daughter, obviously upset, climbed into the car complaining about her class. It seems that, because it was Black History Month, her teacher had chosen to share a little history about black people in America.

"She's so upset that the brown people didn't get paid. I don't know what to do," a desperate Joanna said, endearing herself to me forever. "I took her to McDonald's."

One Happy Meal and music-filled drive later, my daughter arrived intact. But it opened my eyes to how necessary it was for me—and parents like me—to teach our children black history even while the rest of America ignored it.

That was the seminal moment when I began a years-long campaign to lobby for American schools to teach all American history all the time, one America, one history.

As I wrote in the *Detroit Free Press* in 2017: "Rather than acknowledge that America is still dealing with the vestiges of slavery, America has spent centuries trying to make that chapter—and minority history—and black Americans disappear in a miasma of assimilation governed by a curriculum that treats black accomplishments and contributions like minor commercials in a longer, more important narrative.

"If we want a united America, we cannot live in a country that once made it illegal to teach black Americans to read, then spent centuries making it difficult to read about us.

"That Carter G. Woodson, the noted historian, journalist and scholar, was able to get America to accept a Black History Week in 1926 was a stunning and worthy achievement. That the American civil rights movement helped it grow into Black History Month 40 years later was monumental."

That we've come no further is heartbreaking.

And with each passing day, African Americans lose more history, more heritage, more of the information that connects us to one another and to our pasts. The best of our history is disappearing; the best of our present is being diminished. That includes accomplishments by President Barack Obama, the target of some critics who were offended by his election and are attempting to erase his tenure.

I have spent years—and continue to spend days—facing closeted bigots, their Ku Klux Klansmen robes replaced by hooded eyes watching as I enter rooms where they feel I don't belong, try to achieve what they have reserved for their buddies. It. Happens. All. The. Time.

I thought of Mr. Bailum Pitt as I read about the treatment of former slaves post-Emancipation, who couldn't get jobs and sometimes got arrested for petty crimes so they could be sentenced to indentured servitude to pay their legal fines. It was slavery all over again. Douglas Blackmon, in his seminal masterpiece, *Slavery by Another Name*, detailed the 1908 arrest and re-enslavement of Green Cottenham, because, "by 1900, the South's judicial system had been wholly reconfigured to make one of its primary purposes the coercion of African Americans to comply with the social customs and labor demands of whites."

Moreover, he wrote, "African Americans were portrayed by most historians as an almost static component of U.S. society. Their leaders changed with each generation, but the mass of black Americans were depicted as if the freed slaves of 1863 were the same people still not free fifty years later. There was no acknowledgment of the effects of cycle upon cycle of malevolent defeat, of the injury of seeing one generation rise above the cusp of poverty only to be indignantly crushed . . ."

And: "Unlike the victims of the Jewish Holocaust, who were on the whole literate, comparatively wealthy and positioned to record for history the horror that enveloped them, Cottenham and his peers had virtually no capacity to preserve their memories or document their destruction. . . . For the vast majority, no recordings, writings, images or physical descriptions survive."

No capacity to preserve their memories or document their destruction.

Lord, our lost history.

Imagine being a child who reads at age three, decides she wants to be a writer at age eight, and decides she wants to be a journalist at fifteen. Then imagine being that child as she discovers that the more she learns about her classmates' families and history and place in America, the less she knows about her own.

When I was forced to ride a bus across my little hometown to school, all part of a grand experiment to desegregate America on the backs of its children, did anyone really think racists would be less hateful to children? The devotion to that method of attaining equality was so strong that our best and brightest sacrificed their innocents, their children, and the experiment still failed.

I have said many times over the past twenty years that the U.S. Supreme Court's 1954 decision in *Brown v. Board of Education* wasn't the wrong decision but a victorious outcome in the wrong case.

Once again, African Americans were seeking acceptance, searching for an equality that required sitting next to whites in class, on a bus. The brilliant attorney Thurgood Marshall should have argued that America owed its black children, the grandchildren of former slaves, an equal education. We might have gotten it, had we won separate schools with equal resources. Instead, Marshall won the battle but African Americans lost the war. Over the past sixty decades, schools have become as desegregated as they were in the 1950s.

I, like many parents, personally watched it happen.

When I arrived in Louisville, Ky., as an executive at *The Courier-Journal*, my daughter was two. By the time she was ready for kindergarten, and I had studied the public schools to death, I chose one that I felt was appropriate: Samuel Coleridge Taylor Elementary, which was named for the Creole and English composer. As I completed her enrollment forms, one of the reporters from the newsroom came by my office to remind me to enroll her in the "magnet" program, not the "comprehensive" one.

The magnet program was a highly funded special program designed to entice white parents from the suburbs to entrust their children to an inner-city school. The comprehensive program was the lesser-funded section of the building for the black children who lived near the school.

On the first day, my daughter and I entered the brick building, her little hand in mine, and I was overjoyed to see the colorful, newly renovated first floor of the building, which was just blocks from the newspaper.

I was furious, however, when we were directed "upstairs" to older classrooms that hadn't been painted in years, with furniture bought the last time the rooms were painted.

We entered the classroom of my youth, in the segregated school I attended before desegregation, where a beautiful young teacher with the brightest smile said hello to my daughter and apologized for not having textbooks—or enough chairs—and promised things would get better.

My daughter took to her instantly and went over to a hand-me-down kitchen counter set to begin preparing an imaginary breakfast.

"There must be some mistake," I told her. "What's going on downstairs?

"That's the magnet program," she told me.

"That's where my daughter is supposed to be."

The next day, she was—in a classroom run by a German teacher who rarely smiled and who wasn't happy to see her. For every new book and bright toy, there was an unfriendly child and a feeling of dread.

I never should have left her there. I eventually moved her to another school entirely, but the experience fueled her lifelong disdain for school.

It would be the first of many experiences she suffered because she was taught that her skin color mattered.

Every time it happened, I became her. I physically hurt for her. I remember being her.

In January 2017, I gave the keynote address at a community event honoring Dr. Martin Luther King Jr. and told the audience that I remembered, as a young girl, not believing that the year 2000 would be a year. It seemed so far away, so science fictionally impossible. But now, we're 17 years into that new century, and sadly the message that still resonates in Dr. King's words from a half-century ago remains true: "The life of the Negro is still sadly crippled by the manacles of segregation and the chains of discrimination."

I had just returned from Havana, Cuba, where I was blessed to meet the diplomat who helped guide the changes the Obama administration implemented to improve the country's relationship with America. I asked her the same question I asked everyone I met in Cuba: "When will the revolution be over?" She said: "When everything that must be changed, is changed, it will be over."

That is the definition of revolution, the one we have yet to see in America.

America and its citizens will never get over the American Holocaust by pretending that it didn't happen, by accepting a McGraw-Hill textbook claim that "the Atlantic slave trade between the 1500s and 1800s brought millions of workers from Africa to the southern United States to work on agricultural plantations." American will never get over slavery by enabling lesser enslavement through destructive discrimination in the workplace, in medical care, in a ballpark where a black player can be called a racial slur and people rise up to question whether it even happened.

America will not move on from slavery as long as black people are treated as substandard while their best ideas and creativity are stolen decade after decade after decade.

I recalled sitting one night watching *Dreamgirls*, a wonderful film about the rise of a black singing group. But I had to stop watching in the first act when a white group steals a song that was going to make a star of Eddie Murphy's character, James (Thunder) Early. I thought of all the times musical geniuses had their very personas stolen by white performers, who then created awards to laud the thefts.

I remember thinking how many days black Americans must walk a line between civility and rage.

In his December 11, 1964, Nobel lecture a day after receiving the Peace Prize, Dr. Martin Luther King Jr. said: "Every man lives in two realms, the internal and the external. The internal is that realm of spiritual ends expressed in art, literature, morals, and religion. The external is that complex of devices, techniques, mechanisms, and instrumentalities by means of which we live. Our problem today is that we have allowed the internal to become lost in the external."

African Americans are literally losing our religion, our artistry, our morals . . . our morals . . . our morals in efforts to be heard, to feel, to rise. In some instances, that means we are losing our greatness. Many of our children are celebrating the worst of us and ridiculing the best, high-fiving immorality and mocking high achievement by calling those who attain it "white." It is not new. I endured it in high school. But when do we stop?

"Some years ago a famous novelist died," Dr. King continued in that Nobel lecture. "Among his papers was found a list of suggested story plots for future stories, the most prominently underscored being this one: 'A widely separated family inherits a house in which they have to live together.' This is the great new problem of mankind. We have inherited a big house, a great "world house" in which we have to live together—black and white, Easterners and Westerners, Gentiles and Jews, Catholics and Protestants, Moslem and Hindu, a family unduly separated in ideas, culture, and interests who, because we can never again live without each other, must learn, somehow, in this one big world, to live with each other."

Wow. Imagine that.

Imagine how Dr. King would feel now to see the shame of where we are—and to see that we are not much further than we were when he was fighting efforts to disenfranchise voters, doom black children to substandard educations and keep black Americans in lesser-paying jobs.

Dr. King, in his "I Have a Dream" speech, dreamed of a world where America would finally make good on the promissory note it owed black and poor Americans.

I could find no words from him that called for black people to continue seeking permission to be equal in America, or to continue carrying the burden of long-ago subservience.

We have carried the burden for 154 years. It is time to put it down. Only when everyone is free, Fannie Lou Hamer told us, can America be free. And when will we be satisfied?

We won't be, Dr. King said on a hot August day in 1963 on the National Mall in Washington, D.C., "as long as the Negro is the victim of the unspeakable horrors of police brutality. We can never be satisfied as long as our bodies, heavy with the fatigue of travel, cannot gain lodging in the motels of the highways and the hotels of the cities. We cannot be satisfied as long as the Negro's basic mobility is from a smaller ghetto to a larger one."

How can we live with the knowledge that, had Dr. King lived, he might be making that same speech before the new National Museum of African American History and Culture, that the financial and educational and housing gaps between blacks and whites remain—and our rights to vote and change things are threatened every election?

We must stop seeking permission to vote, which means we cannot allow North Carolina or Florida or Texas or Michigan to disenfranchise voters.

We must stop seeking permission to be educated, which means we cannot just hope for equal schools for African American children, but must create what our children need.

We must call out those who aid and abet a system that continues to treat African Americans like second-class citizens or enslaves them in prisons in numbers too heinous to continue to just count. And we must stop letting off the hook those who allow discrimination by ignoring it.

The emotional bondage that replaced the physical bondage may be worse. America didn't just steal the freedom of the enslaved. It stole our stories.

As I wrote in the *Free Press* during the annual truncated celebration of black history:

"When we do not teach a united history that details the incredible journey of all Americans, we are not teaching our children about the best of all of our people. We are teaching our children that America was built only by white Americans, that it was their heroics and passion that made our current lives possible. But what is lost is teaching them to see black people as people, as heroes, as builders, as standard-bearers who helped create America.

"Black Americans have spent too long being portrayed mostly as victims set free by a benevolent president shot to death at age fifty-six, two years after signing the most important executive order of his life."

It is time to accept that we can no longer treat black history and achievement like a novelty we occasionally acknowledge. The annual King celebration, where we pull out the "I Have a Dream" speech, just won't do.

We have spent centuries disappearing the black American story rather than recognizing that there is no American story without black Americans. Now it is time to chart a new course and help end the racial discord that has become as much an American hallmark as our national anthem and our flag.

America wasn't always about slavery. America became about slavery because it made building America easier.

But since Emancipation, millions of African Americans have spent a century and a half trying to fit in, sometimes abandoning our heritage to be successful, hiding our culture to be accepted, seeking permission to live free—all while carrying the burden of a second-class citizenship.

We don't need permission to be great. We don't need permission to be free.

Slavery is over. Why can't we just get over it?

Chile, please. We will get over it when it no longer exists, when America acknowledges our greatness. And that burden of shame and rejection and diminishment and questioning by ourselves and others?

We can lay that burden down.

THE ARMOR WE STILL NEED

A'Lelia Bundles

I still can feel the sting. Prickly flares of embarrassment radiate from my ribs. A half-century later, I am isolated and hot. A half-century later, I also am clear that this fiery shame is not justified. But as a teenager, I do not know how to extinguish it. I have no weapons for the battle.

It is the fall of 1968. I am in my high school American history class, in an affluent suburb of Indianapolis. I am the only black student in the classroom, in an overwhelmingly white public school, seated at a desk in the center row, halfway down the aisle.

The day's topic is the Civil War.

The teacher is a middle-aged white man whose name I struggle to remember. In my old yearbook, I scan photographs of social studies faculty. I shudder when I see the pinched face of the government teacher who was also chairman of the local American Legion's so-called Americanism Committee. Then I smirk because he tried—without success—to have me expelled for wearing an antiwar armband.

When I find my history instructor, I see that he is smiling. Was he oblivious during those moments while I churned inside? Did his sense of curiosity cause him to question the text? Did it even matter that I was in the room? I couldn't have been invisible, so was I inconsequential? Did he mull over how to present such fraught subject matter?

On this day, we are reading from the textbook. My eyes lock on a section titled "Negro Slavery." It is the first time this semester I have seen a reference to people of African descent. The boldface letters blare from the page.

What I remember from that chapter is this: "Slaves" —not "enslaved people," as scholars now prefer to say, but "slaves" —were "contented" and well cared for by their kind and benevolent masters.

Years later, a friend helps me track down the textbook. I am stunned all over again when I read this sentence in Henry Wilkinson Bragdon and Samuel Proctor McCutchen's *History of a Free People*: "Once slaves had been put to work on American plantations they were seldom cruelly treated, since it was to the interest of the master to keep them healthy and contented."

Yes, they conceded, slavery was "a horrible episode in the story of 'man's inhumanity to man,'" but "the freedman was sometimes worse off than the slave."

Once again, I am back in that class, paralyzed and hot. I know in my soul that this paragraph is a lie. I have a feeling, but insufficient facts. Intuition, but no evidence. On that day, without my own research, I am defenseless and without allies.

I don't yet know about resistance and revolt. Not one of my textbooks has included Nat Turner and Harriet Tubman. Ida B. Wells and Frederick Douglass are absent from the curriculum.

The teacher lets the text do the talking. He is a member of the Sons of the American Revolution with no inclination to doubt white male entitlement and supremacy. He has faith in the version of history he studied in graduate school. He accepts the notion that my black ancestors were "contented" with being enslaved. By teaching this, he also teaches that his white ancestors—and by proxy, all white people—are free of any responsibility for the privileged status they inherit or enjoy. His ignorance of a more nuanced interpretation of 19th century reality means my classmates and I are being mis-educated.

So years later, when I read Jack Kelly's 2015 *Pittsburgh Post-Gazette* column absolving his white readers from any complicity in our nation's racial conundrum, I cringe. But I am not at all surprised. I know he is not writing for me, but for people who have the luxury of going through life without having to think about race.

"Slavery was horrible, but no black American living today has suffered from it," he wrote, with eerie echoes of Bragdon and McCutchen. "Most are better off than if their ancestors had remained in Africa."

What I have learned about Jack Kelly—who was born John Michael Kelly in 1947 in Minneapolis—is that we both grew up as Midwesterners. He graduated from the University of Wisconsin in 1970, the same year I graduated from North Central High School. He served in Vietnam as a Marine. I protested the war.

Our demographic similarities and differences make me wonder if he might have found kinship with the conservative teenage boys in my class. I can't help thinking that our high school history lessons, if not from the same textbook, were informed by the same mid-20th-century approach to American history.

The sad thing is that by 2015, Kelly had lived long enough to educate himself on the matter. What he failed to grasp is this: we have no expectation or desire for him or his readers to carry any personal guilt for what a slave ship captain did two hundred years ago. But what is reasonable to expect of a columnist for a major daily is that he stop denying the continuing impact of legal and societal barriers that were erected after slavery was abolished.

On April 4, 1968, a few months before that history class, I was elected vice president of my school's student council. Later that day, Dr. Martin Luther King Jr. was assassinated in Memphis. Celebration quickly turned to anguish.

The next morning, I learned that a few white parents had called the school to complain about the election. For the most part, teachers and school administrators, who had mentored and nurtured me, also shielded me from that nasty parental bigotry. The next spring, when I ran for student council president, there were uncomfortable undercurrents around race and gender. There had never been a black female in that position. Another candidate who had been involved in student government was my opponent. The principal's son, who had little previous leadership involvement, ran for vice president. During my campaign speech, I was heckled by a handful of students who booed from a corner of the auditorium. I lost by a few votes.

I don't remember any particular sense of sadness or defeat, perhaps because I understood exactly what had been engineered. I moved on. I spent part of the summer at a camp for high school journalists at Northwestern University, in a decidedly more progressive environment. I began my senior year as co-editor of the newspaper and had my say through my columns. With a white male classmate, I co-founded a Human Relations Council to navigate racial tensions and build alliances in a 3,400-member student body that was less than 5 percent black.

It was a year of turmoil for America and a year of radicalization for me. I began a journey of self-discovery and self-education. At some point, I read W. E. B. Du Bois's *The Souls of Black Folk*. That slim volume was an elixir that offered me a combination of intellectual fireworks, historical facts and much-needed affirmation.

These words from Du Bois—"The problem of the 20th century is the problem of the color line, the relation of the darker to the lighter races of men in Asia and Africa, in America and the islands of the sea"—unlocked a world and a perspective I'd never heard in a classroom. His brief account of America from 1861 to 1872, of Reconstruction and of the Freedmen's Bureau was the primer I'd been missing.

When he described the "unreconciled strivings" of being both black and American, it felt as if he had come through the pages to provide the ammunition I'd lacked the year before:

"It is a peculiar sensation, this double-consciousness, this sense of always looking at one's self through the eyes of others, of measuring one's soul by the tape of a world that looks on in amused contempt and pity."

What I did not know then, but what I surely have come to understand, is that all those moments—the history class, the student council elections, my introduction to Du Bois—would become fodder and sustenance for the books I now write, the causes I support and the issues that continue to matter to me.

What I understand now is that the contributions—the blood, sweat and tears—of women and people of color were erased from American history lessons, sometimes intentionally, sometimes inadvertently.

Inconvenient truths unmask America's imperfections.

Examples of genocide and exclusion expose contradictions.

But rather than embrace the challenges that arose in the quest "to form a more perfect union," America chose to render mute and make invisible the atrocities and blunders that exist throughout our national narrative. Rather than air the troublesome facts, the official response almost always has been to smother and deny.

Half-truths and outright lies provided the justification for local, state and federal laws that determined where we lived, the schools we attended, the loans we got (or more often didn't get), the generational wealth we were unable to build. Slavery ended, but Black Codes and fugitive slave laws were replaced by Jim Crow legislation that codfied racially based discrimination. What had been incubated, born, and nurtured during slavery continued to grow and thrive long after the Emancipation Proclamation. Rather than equality of opportunity when the 13th Amendment was ratified, African Americans faced another century of underfunded schools, discriminatory housing policies, and murderous voter suppression.

Despite the record and the evidence, these realities are not acknowledged often enough in American history classes. In Texas—where the state school board is notoriously averse to progressive ideas—textbooks still equivocate about slavery's role as the cause of the Civil War.

In 2015, a Houston parent named Roni Dean-Burren found herself embroiled in a national controversy after her son told her about his McGraw-Hill geography textbook's immigration chapter. Absent was any mention of slave ships and involuntary servitude. Instead, the Africans who arrived in America from the 1500s through the 1800s were described as "workers." What began as a protest on her Facebook page resulted in the publisher's commitment to revise the text.

The effort to sanitize history persists, but it should be made clear that slavery was neither benign nor charitable. It was a brutal, often sadistic, form of domination over the bodies and minds of people who were kidnapped, whipped, beaten, shackled, and raped. Generations of human beings toiled without pay or legal rights. Enslaved Americans were listed in their owners' inventory ledgers alongside cattle and farm equipment. They most certainly were not voluntary immigrants, willing workers, or contented plantation residents.

Slavery and the act of auctioning men, women, and children were essential to the development of American capitalism and to trade with Europe, Africa, the Caribbean, and South America. The wealth of the nation depended upon uncompensated labor, which enriched not just planters but universities, banks, textile mills, ship owners, and the insurance companies that held policies on their bodies. Recent research has revealed that Georgetown University would have gone bankrupt in 1838 had its trustees not sold 272 enslaved people to settle its debts.

Forty of the 56 signers of the Declaration of Independence owned other people. Twelve presidents were slaveholders at some point during their lives. When the first shot of the Civil War was fired at Fort Sumter in April 1861, the value of America's four million enslaved people exceeded $3 billion, or more than the nation's banks, railroads, mills and factories combined.

This story has been told for decades by a small group of historians. Du Bois's *Black Reconstruction in America*, first published in 1935, was a corrective to the Confederate-centric version of the brief era when black men first had the right to vote. John Hope Franklin, Eric Foner,

Nell Irvin Painter, and Ira Berlin, among others, have built upon his work and expanded the canon. More recently, books like Edward E. Baptist's *The Half Has Never Been Told: Slavery and the Making of American Capitalism* and Annette Gordon-Reed's *The Hemingses of Monticello* have delved into slavery's pivotal role in the earliest days of America. Craig Steven Wilder's *Ebony and Ivy: Race, Slavery, and the Troubled History of America's Universities*, Michelle Alexander's *The New Jim Crow* and Ta-Nehisi Coates's *Atlantic* article "The Case for Reparations" have connected the dots between the past and present in ways that inform our current critique of race, education, white supremacy, income inequality, police misconduct, incarceration, and a vast, unfinished social justice agenda.

I wish I had confidence to believe that this knowledge would be incorporated into textbooks that are now being written.

I see myself in that classroom 50 years ago and wish I had known about Phillis Wheatley's Revolutionary War-era poetry, or about the five thousand African Americans who served in George Washington's Continental Army. I wish I had known that one of those free men of color was my great-great-great-great-grandfather Ishmael Roberts, who traveled to Valley Forge with Col. Abraham Sheppard's 10th North Carolina Regiment.

I still can feel the sting of shame that was triggered by a false narrative and by a teacher who made no effort to correct the record. I remember unflattering textbook references to carpetbaggers and scalawags, who temporarily interfered with the former Confederates' return to political power in the South. But why was there nothing in the curriculum about men like my great-great-grandfather Henderson B. Robinson, who was elected to the Arkansas state legislature and who served as sheriff of predominantly black Phillips County during Reconstruction?

Had I known the story of his mother, Delphia Hendry—who successfully sued for her freedom in Tennessee in 1839—I would have been able to speak up in my high school history class to refute the notion of contented slaves.

In graduate school, I began researching the life of one of my great-great-grandmothers, Madam C. J. Walker, an early 20th-century entrepreneur, who never appeared in my textbooks. She'd started life as Sarah Breedlove in 1867 on the same Delta, La., plantation where her parents had been enslaved. Her family minister, who had been a state senator, was chased at gunpoint from Madison Parish in 1879 by so-called white Redeemers determined to take the state back from black voters and elected officials.

In 1888, she followed her brothers to St. Louis, where she worked as a washerwoman for the next eighteen years until she developed an ointment that healed dandruff and scalp infections. Using the name of her third husband, Charles Joseph Walker, she began marketing her Madam Walker's Wonderful Hair Grower. By the time she died in 1919, she had become a millionaire philanthropist, patron of the arts and activist who provided jobs for thousands of African American women and financial support for the NAACP's anti-lynching initiative.

To broaden our understanding of slavery's legacy, we must go beyond the 19th century and even the success stories of exceptional people like Madam Walker. To equip future generations of students of all races, we must examine the federal policies of the early 20th century and probe how those policies still drive our political discourse.

It's shocking to learn that even the New Deal that helped America recover from the Great Depression was rigged and riddled with racial bias. Social Security benefits initially were denied to farm laborers and maids, who made up two-thirds of the South's black workforce in the 1930s. The Federal Housing Administration's Home Owners' Loan Corporation created maps in 239 American cities that drew red lines around poor—and mostly minority—neighborhoods. Inside those "residential security" zones, banks denied mortgages. Over time, that intentional disinvestment meant homes owned by black families failed to build equity at the same rate as comparable homes owned by white families. Less equity meant less wealth for subsequent generations.

The Federal Highway Act of 1944 compounded the damage by funding freeways that indiscriminately cut through the heart of dozens of historically black neighborhoods. Churches, businesses, schools, restaurants, stores, and health centers were bulldozed or by-passed. The new roads were designed to provide easy access to down-town business districts for the mostly white families who had moved to the booming post-World War II suburbs. Black communities became collateral damage. They have never recovered.

In 1957, when my parents were ready to buy a new home in an all-black development of newly constructed residences in an Indianapolis suburb, they couldn't get a loan from any of the city's large banks. Both were college graduates and business executives. Our neighbors were doctors, teachers, coaches, plumbers, entrepreneurs, realtors, nurses, ministers, architects, insurance salesmen, and carpenters. Many of the fathers were veterans of World War II and the Korean War who were eligible for the G.I. Bill's home loan guaranty—in other words, people who should have had no trouble qualifying for mortgages. Instead, they went to Mammoth Life Insurance, a black-owned firm then based in Louisville, Kentucky, for their loans.

Despite the roadblocks, our parents and our ancestors persisted. That resilience is as much a part of our legacy as the struggle. Despite the tripwires, they brought their talents to American science, business, technology, culture, education and the military.

Until we incorporate these truths into our history lessons, the American story will remain inaccurate, incomplete and dishonest. Yet another generation will be taught that black Americans—as well as other people of color—have played no role in the nation's development. They will convince themselves that the only "real Americans" are white Americans. They will believe that inequality happened by coincidence and not by design. They will learn to deny the reality that systemic, institutional racism is baked into our American DNA.

Although I rarely think of that painful hour in my high school history class, the experience planted seeds that still grow. Five decades later, I wake up each morning determined to dig up the details and expand the boundaries of the American narrative. I now write biographies about the amazing and complex women in my family. I now write the kind of books I wish had been written for me.

It is my mission to tell the stories that will give future generations the armor I did not have on that day when I needed it.

It is the armor they still need.

A MILITARY FAMILY, DESCENDED FROM SLAVES

Benét J. Wilson

I come from a military family.

My father, Dr. Bennie J. Wilson III, a professor at the University of Texas-San Antonio, served in the U.S. Air Force from 1965 to 1995 and retired as a colonel.

His father, Bennie J. Wilson, served in the Army Air Corps and the Air Force from 1942 to 1969, retiring as a chief warrant officer in 1969.

There have been men like my father and grandfather serving this country for centuries.

It is a proud history that defies the irony of colonialists fighting to escape from British rule even as they held blacks against their will.

The history of African Americans in the military predates the United States as we know it. By the 1770s, the original thirteen colonies were home to more than five hundred thousand blacks, the vast majority of them slaves. During that same time, America had 217,000 soldiers, while between five thousand and eight thousand slaves were soldiers, according to Edward Ayres, a historian at the American Revolution Museum at Yorktown, in Virginia.

Imagine that. Abigail Adams did.

"It always appeared a most iniquitous scheme to me to fight ourselves for what we are daily robbing and plundering from those who have as good a right to freedom as we have," Adams, the wife of future president John Adams, wrote in 1774—several years after Crispus Attucks, a black soldier, became "the first person killed in the Boston massacre and the first American casualty in the American Revolutionary War." Adams's acknowledgment, in *Dearest Friend: A Life of Abigail Adams*, has always stayed with me.

Thousands of slaves enlisted in the military to fight for freedom from the rule of King George III. But some were fighting for so much more. As the war dragged on, the colonies that made up the Continental Army, struggling to find enough men to enlist, began recruiting slaves, promising them freedom once the war was over. Slaves played major roles in big battles, including those at Lexington and Bunker Hill.

But by 1776, it was clear that the dreams of the nearly eight thousand slaves who had fought for the new nation in the hope of obtaining their own freedom would be dashed. When the Founding Fathers wrote the Declaration of Independence, they learned that that famous line promising "life, liberty and the pursuit of happiness" did not apply to them. And the passage that Thomas Jefferson wrote attacking slavery was savaged by delegates from South Carolina and Georgia as well as some Northern delegates representing merchants. The passage, which was removed but should be required reading, said:

"He has waged cruel war against human nature itself, violating its most sacred rights of life and liberty in the persons of a distant people who never offended him, captivating & carrying them into slavery in another hemisphere, or to incur miserable death in their transportation thither. This piratical warfare, the opprobrium of infidel powers, is the warfare of the Christian King of Great Britain. Determined to keep open a market where men should be bought & sold, he has prostituted his negative for suppressing every legislative attempt to prohibit or to restrain this execrable commerce. And that this assemblage of horrors might want no fact of distinguished die, he is now exciting those very people to rise in arms among us, and to purchase that liberty of which he has deprived them, by murdering the people on whom he has obtruded them: thus paying off former crimes committed again the Liberties of one people, with crimes which he urges them to commit against the lives of another."

During the War of 1812, slaves again enlisted in the military in hopes of being freed after their service. "In the end, the War of 1812 did not provide greater opportunities or equality for free blacks as they anticipated, nor did it initiate a wave of emancipation for enslaved Americans seeking freedom," according to a report by the National Park Service. "They would find themselves wedged between slavery and freedom, and between race discrimination and egalitarianism. Their patriotic efforts had not reshaped white minds about what role they should play in society, and public memories of the war largely ignored their contributions."

The park service notes that "new prejudicial racial distinctions replaced class differences among blacks and destroyed once and for all the optimism of the Revolutionary era. For African Americans, the 'forgotten war' delayed their quest for equality and freedom."

The original intent of the Civil War was to avoid the splintering of the Union. But slavery became a major part of the battle, with thousands of slaves escaping to the North and joining the Union Army, hoping this would be the battle that would result in their freedom. Nearly two hundred thousand slaves fought in the Civil War, and the U.S. Colored Troops were lauded for their service in major battles, with many members awarded the Medal of Honor. These units of Colored Troops were credited with helping the Union win the war.

On December 6, 1865, the United States ratified the 13th Amendment to the Constitution, which outlawed the practice of slavery and effectively freed more than three million slaves.

The 14th Amendment, granting the Constitution's full protections to the newly freed slaves, and the 15th Amendment, guaranteeing that a citizen's right to vote would not be denied "on account of race, color, or previous condition of servitude," were also ratified after the war.

This series of amendments brought about Reconstruction, which was designed to integrate former slaves into American society. But Reconstruction was short-lived as Southern states enacted "black codes" and Jim Crow laws aimed at placing certain prewar restrictions on activities such as voting and freedom of movement back on the newly emancipated blacks.

But despite these setbacks, blacks were still patriotic, and saw military service as a way to gain a semblance of freedom and opportunity for themselves and their families. They played major roles in the Spanish-American War, World War I, World War II, the Korean War, and the Vietnam War.

In an interview with me, my father, Dr. Bennie J. Wilson III, said: "At the start of World War II, patriotism was rampant and blacks and other minorities raced to join in the war effort. My father was intensely loyal to the United States. He saw the military as a chance to serve his country and support his family."

My grandfather, Bennie J. Wilson, enlisted, did his basic training in San Antonio, Texas, and entered the Army Air Corps as a private. At the time, the military was still segregated. "During those times, the leadership was white officers and black and white noncommissioned officers," or NCOs, my father said. "Because leadership among black NCOs to help run these units was sparse, my father, seen as a leader, went from private to master sergeant, the highest NCO rank, in only 11 months."

After the war, the Army Air Corps turned into the U.S. Air Force and my grandfather became a warrant officer. "They were not commissioned officers, but warrant officers were saluted by enlisted men and shared most of the benefits of officers," my father said.

My father grew up on bases around the world as an Air Force brat, and wanted to follow in my grandfather's footsteps, so he enrolled in the ROTC program at San Jose State College. He was commissioned as a second lieutenant in 1965.

My father was originally selected for assignment at Warner-Robins Air Force Base in Georgia. I recall him telling me that his father would not let him go to Georgia because the base was in the Deep South, which was still segregated. This was true despite President Harry Truman signing an executive order to desegregate the military on July 26, 1948.

"My father felt that going to Warner-Robins would hurt my career because there were still too many segregationists in the military," my dad said. "He had a lot of experience and I trusted him. He contacted the base commander at Offutt Air Force Base near Omaha, Nebraska, someone he had worked for, and asked him to find a place for me there."

The military changed during my grandfather's career, becoming, as he put it, one of the leaders in equal opportunity in the workplace.

"Early on, they did deny promotions to blacks, along with access to the choice assignments needed for career upward mobility," he said. "Until [fighter pilot] Daniel 'Chappie' James became the first four-star general in the Air Force in 1975, it was still a struggle."

My father took full advantage of his opportunities: from plum assignments in England and Belgium to being tapped by the Air Force Institute of Technology (A.F.I.T.), which oversees graduate and continuing education for military and civilian employees, to getting his master's degree at the University of Rochester and a PhD in education from Auburn University. Wilson accomplished much in his military career, helping to mentor and train a generation of black NCOs and officers. He ended his service to his country as the interim commandant of A.F.I.T.

I considered a career in the military; I went so far as to request an application for the U.S. Air Force Academy. But I decided on a career as a journalist.

Of all the things I appreciate about the opportunities afforded me through my father's and grandfather's service, one of the greatest was my choice not to serve.

I am the beneficiary of their service, just as the descendants in every family carry the benefits or burdens of their history.

The sacrifices made by black soldiers, ranging from slaves dying for colonists' freedom from British tyranny while living under American tyranny to former soldiers becoming compatriots in the civil rights movement, made clear that freedom was paramount.

But today, some black Americans are joining the military less because of patriotism and more to get away from chronic unemployment and a lack of opportunities in their communities. Some take advantage of what military service can offer—education, a career, a way to support their families—while others serve and return to the same places they had hoped to escape.

That American textbooks and leaders downplay the sacrifices and patriotism of black soldiers in wars that shaped America, going back to the Revolutionary War, is shameful. That black soldiers, in spite of their plight, helped fulfill a promise of freedom 240 years in the making is worth celebrating. While still far from perfect, the military is still giving black Americans the chance to carve paths to what was promised in the Declaration of Independence: life, liberty and the pursuit of happiness.

As we continue to strive for all three, their service is something we descendants should never forget.

REMNANTS OF SURVIVAL

BLACK WOMEN AND LEGACIES OF DEFIANCE

Charlene A. Carruthers

I imagine that Audre Lorde—black lesbian feminist, writer, and intellectual—had the histories of black women who made it through the Middle Passage in mind when she published "A Litany for Survival" in 1978. The repetitive declaration throughout the poem, "We were never meant to survive," describes a difficult truth about the legacies of chattel slavery. Our foremothers survived kidnappings, the trauma of rape as a normal form of control, and indefinite bondage across the Americas as the status quo. The survival of generations of enslaved African people, particularly women, and their descendants makes my existence possible. I am because they were.

This became clear for me as I stood in the "female slave dungeon" at Elmina Castle in Cape Coast, Ghana, in the summer of 2015. I was certain of three things before entering the grounds: (1) I would refuse to join a tour with any white people; (2) I was not emotionally prepared for what was to come; (3) I would be able to go home, unlike my ancestors who were raped, tortured, killed and kidnapped centuries ago.

I was with a friend and her family. We joined a small group that walked around the main courtyard and listened to a general history of Elmina Castle, also known as St. George's Castle. The tour guide was knowledgeable and pleasant enough. He spoke frankly about the violence inflicted on the enslaved Africans brought there. He shared that Christians held church services in rooms directly above the dungeons where enslaved Africans were kept before transport. He walked us around the five-hundred-year-old structure speaking with clarity and not much embellishment for a story in which even the basic details had the power to strike the soul.

Suddenly, I felt the floor fall from beneath me, and my spirit cracked as we walked into the female slave dungeon. I stood no more than thirty seconds in that place where women were once packed in, waiting for transport to a slave ship (or the captain's sleeping quarters) before I broke into tears.

I was sick that day and could not smell anything. But I felt that moment. I felt the weight of what happened in that place. A pain sat in my gut and across my chest cavity, heavy with the weight of what I know and what I continue to learn about what it means to be a black queer/lesbian woman in this world. I imagined the fear they felt, those women, the longing and loss they experienced. My intellectual wandering stopped when we reached the captain's quarters.

I could not enter. The tour guide explained how this was the place where enslaved African women were brought and raped. My curiosity vanished after learning how the legacy of narrow and prescriptive definitions of womanhood, disposability, commodification, and reproductive injustice continues even to this day.

The makers of the United States of America benefited from the violence and greed of the slave trade. The remnants of those choices have created a culture, economy and society where the autonomy of our bodies is not guaranteed—and to be anything besides white, cisgender, or heterosexual is deemed deviant and vulnerable to violent domination. That culture lives through systemic sexual violence, reproductive injustice, and other forms of violence. I come from those women—the ones who made it and those who did not make it out of the darkness, filth, and violence of the female slave dungeons. There, the horrors of slavery reproduced the worst of humanity—including the roots of today's pervasive mistreatment and dehumanization of black women in the Americas.

Black women have long known that our bodies and our children are not fully our own. As result, we have fought fiercely for self-determination, self-defense, and collective responsibility.

We should look to what happened to Korryn Gaines, the twenty-three-year-old mother killed by a SWAT team in her home while defending herself and her son's life in 2016. She was in her apartment, according to an account in *The Washington Post*, when three Baltimore County police officers showed up to serve a warrant for failing to appear in court on a traffic ticket. Officers said they entered the apartment with a key and found her sitting on the floor with her five-year-old son in one arm and a shotgun in the other. She raised the shotgun, they said, so they fired. Her son was slightly injured. She was killed. She was twenty-three.

Rosa Parks, well known for her arrest for refusing to give up her seat on a Montgomery, Ala., bus, should be as known for her years of grassroots organizing to end sexual violence against black women. The Montgomery bus boycott, a crucial weapon in the U.S. civil rights movement, was the result of years of organizing that Parks, and other women, including Jo Ann Robinson, led in defense of black women. As a matter of fact, it was Robinson, a teacher and president of the Women's Political Council in Montgomery, who conceived the idea of the boycott.

What I know for sure is that this country was not designed to love or care for black women. Any semblance of dignity we possess today was fought for and maintained by those who imagined that another world was possible. We are because of those who came before us—both the oppressed and the oppressors. I come from the "race women" of the early 20th century, from Rosa Parks, Fannie Lou Hamer, Marsha P. Johnson. I come from the liberators, from Harriet Tubman, who led a successful raid at the Combahee River in 1863, where seven hundred enslaved Africans were liberated. I come from the daughters of the women who migrated North and lived in the urban ghettos of Chicago.

I've carried something unshakeable within my consciousness, and my body, about the histories of black people whose lineages were crafted through the trans-Atlantic slave trade since I began to learn of its horrors. Not everyone survived and all suffered trauma beyond what I've known in my own life.

From the slave dungeons of Elmina Castle to Korryn Gaines's Baltimore County apartment—black women continue to live under the heel of practices, beliefs and laws that codify our status as sub-human and commodity. Our defiance is an insistence of humanity and expression of the black radical imagination. This was summed up beautifully by Miss Major Griffin-Gracy, a black transwoman activist and leader, who declared: "I'm still fucking here."

We are still here, resisting, loving, and dreaming.

QUIET DEFIANCE
Aku Kadogo

Here's the thing: Post-slavery bigotry was such an incessant cancer that it invaded even the most idyllic of black lives.

To understand what happened, you need to know my father, Donald Vest. My father was a man who went through his entire life with his inner child intact. He laughed easily, played with us as though he was one of our siblings, whistled while he walked, heartily greeted strangers, and generally seemed to love life.

But he also could be cuttingly sarcastic and offered serious one-liners on any number of topics; every family member being in possession of their own "Don Vestism." These one-liners were also guides for how to navigate the world he was sending his children out to face. The one I carry with me is, "The best revenge is to live well." And I like to think I have!

But I finally learned—like the young child in *Life Is Beautiful*, whose father hides from him the horror of their lives in a Nazi concentration camp—that all was not as it seemed.

For instance, I didn't know until I was in my fifties—and my father was in his seventies—that he had attended a predominantly white private school from kindergarten through twelfth grade in Ypsilanti,

Mich., where he was born. Because I saw my dad comfortable in any situation, I never once wondered how or why he was able to do that.

He delighted us as children with his gymnastic prowess and tumbling ability. He was a member of the gymnastics team at Michigan State University, which he attended from 1948 to 1952. He was the first African American gymnast in the Big Ten Conference, and the only African American on the gymnastics team during his tenure at M.S.U.

But what he kept from us was the ugly side of his experiences, the racism he wanted us to never experience. There was an occasion when the team was invited to an exclusive club in Detroit, and my dad wasn't allowed to go. I have a photograph from that visit, the team members decked out in their dress sport attire and lined up in neat rows. However, in the same photograph, my dad is poised for action in his sporting gear. His picture is pasted into the team photograph, creating a glaring contrast.

The picture represents his protest of the unfairness and offensiveness of being excluded from the Detroit visit. He chose not to attend the photo shoot. But the coach, embracing the team's integration, hoping to maintain team spirit, and affirming his decision to accept my father onto the team in the first place, pasted my dad's picture onto the photo, creating the conspicuous contrast but featuring the entire team.

Yes, slavery forced people a century later to live the lie of freedom, the lie of equality. That picture represented the coach's efforts to move into the future, but also was a stark and heartbreaking reminder of how hard it is to move away from the past.

Living in those two worlds has been a way of life for African Americans for centuries. But the thing about my dad is that he controlled how we viewed those worlds. He taught me to do it as well.

I remember a time we were at a hotel swimming pool, and apparently all the white people had gotten out of the pool when we got in. We didn't notice. We said, "Hey! We've got the whole pool!" He didn't say anything, and I didn't know for years. He told us when we were adults. I went through life like that. He taught us: "Do what you want. Go where you think you want. You belong where you stand on this earth!"

Now, that is something I tell my students because the earth doesn't belong to any one group of people. I told a student that once at her senior celebration, and she just burst into tears. This game of racism is very real, it dictates us all the time. There is a part of me that wonders, How *did* people imagine themselves out of slavery? How did that happen? Because they must have had a mighty will. If that is all you know, how do you envision more? My father helped me envision more. He didn't let us see what could have held us back.

Of course, the enslavement—the emotional, mental, and cultural enslavement—is real. It is real now. But it is in the minds of both blacks and whites—the enslaved and those who enslave.

So what do we do now? As George Clinton would say: "Free your mind, and your ass will follow."

In working with young people, one hopes to instill in them a way to reclaim their agency. We have to reach our young people to free their imaginations. I know there are things they deal with. Black kids deal with very real racism: the prison system, the breakup of black families, redlining. Take Detroit. All the white people who are moving to Detroit understand how black people have been intentionally marginalized for years, facing redlining, auto insurance rates that are four and five times higher than they're used to paying. Now all the white people come to town and say, "You pay real high car insurance here!" Duh, yes. That is what black people endured.

There is so much intent to break us all the time. Welcome to the world of intentionality against a people.

But, and this is important: One can be broken by it or handle it the way my father did.

Clearly, there was such a huge impact on my parents' ability to move in the world. But they did what they had to do. That's what moves me through the world now. Yes, it's work. It's daily work. But my father did that work and did not let racism steal his joy. He didn't let it steal our joy.

And there will come moments that shore you up, that remind you that the work is worth it.

There was another time that segregation reared its ugly head with my father's gymnastics team. On a trip to Chicago, they entered a restaurant where my dad was refused service. The coach and all of his white teammates got up and walked out in solidarity.

That photo of my father with those young men and that coach stand for those times that he had to live in those two worlds. It represents so much more than a sport.

That photo was on exhibit at Michigan State University for a number of years. And Dad would continue to visit the gymnastics coach on his trips back to Michigan State for the duration of his life. Always aware and defiant, Dad offered this bit of advice: "Beat 'em at their own game"—whoever they are.

LIVING WITHOUT A BEGINNING

Patrice Gaines

I was watching the reality television show *America's Next Top Model*, where beautiful young women compete for a modeling contract. On a December 2016 episode, a model named Binta, a native of Gambia, got into a shouting match with a young black model named Giah.

The models were talking about race and the Black Lives Matter movement. Binta says she understands such issues and has an understanding of black history.

"The history is not true!" Giah says. "Everything is a lie! You know where you come from! We don't know where we come from!"

"You come from Africa!" Binta insists.

"No, we do not!" Giah responds, adamant.

"Yes, you do!" screams Binta.

Then, as another black American model agrees with Giah, a frustrated Binta asks, "Then where the fuck do you come from?"

"We do not know who we are," the other model says. "That's why we are African Americans."

Alone later, Giah speaks into a "confessional camera": "We trying to explain to her [Binta] that we are Americans, that we do not identify with Africans because we are black Americans. We are the only people who don't know where we come from."

Imagine not having a beginning for 400 years.

No one has ever been able to explain to me the harm that is caused by not knowing how you started, where you started, who your people are. It is the reason there was such celebration among blacks in 1976 when Alex Haley's book "Roots: The Saga of an American Family" was published. Haley told the story of his family's history, going back to slavery, about his ancestor Kunta Kinte being kidnapped in Gambia. The youth arrived in the province of Maryland in 1767 and was sold as a slave.

Haley was a seventh-generation descendant of Kunta Kinte, his research proving that, with determination, black Americans could trace the jagged waterways back to a beginning place. The year after publication, the book was adapted as a television miniseries and drew a record-breaking 130 million viewers. But the story struck emotions worldwide, proof that this search to find "home" is universal. The book was published in 37 languages, and Haley said that the most emotional day of his life was September 29, 1967, when he stood at the site in Annapolis, Md., where Kunta Kinte arrived from Africa in chains 200 years earlier. Haley's search and Pulitzer Prize–winning literature was spurned by the heartache of not being able to point to an exact spot on a world map and say, as many of my white friends do, "That is where my family is from."

This "homelessness" of the spirit ripples through decades of human living, causing unseen damage. But we humans like our harm to be concrete. We like to have physical scars and measurable pain. I offer up the self-hatred of many black people, which manifests in uncountable ways in La La Land. For many, not knowing where you begin means not caring how you end.

I wrote in my book *Moments of Grace* that "during my period of horrific self-hatred, I had one huge desire, one goal that kept me alive: I wanted to be somebody. Not a writer, a reporter, or an author. . . . I wanted to believe I mattered to this earth. I wanted to believe I had worth."

The fear of being nobody seeps into your bones and blood and destroys you in ways scientists have yet to identify. Part of being some-body is having a beginning, knowing where to point to on a map and say, "This is where my people started."

As a teenager, I prayed to God to let that place be farther away than North Carolina or South Carolina, to restore to me a sense of home that slavery snatched away.

I have always tried to satisfy my questions with spiritual answers, even when I was in elementary school in Beaufort, S.C., and white kids on their shiny yellow buses passed me yelling "Nigger!"

My father was a Marine and our family had just transferred to Beaufort from Quantico, Va., where my best friends were white. So I told God to explain, "Why are these new white kids differ-ent from Charlotte and Lucy?" Charlotte and Lucy were my best friends in Virginia—and they were little white girls. I knew I was the same brown girl with buckteeth and crinkly braids that I had been before the moving van carried my twin bed 525 miles south. But for some reason, these new white children didn't adore me the way Charlotte and Lucy did.

I was not satisfied with the answers God gave me, which seemed to me at the time to be no answer at all.

Some fifteen years later, as a single mother, I still searched for answers. My quest led me to a book called *A Course in Miracles*, a "self-study spiritual thought system" that "teaches that the way to universal love and peace—or remembering God—is by undoing guilt through forgiving others. The course thus focuses on the healing of relationships and making them holy."

At the time, I wore a big Afro and was surrounded by black peo-ple who hated white people. I secretly fluctuated in my feelings be-cause of Charlotte and Lucy. I knew that I could love little blond girls—and this one fact separated me from many of my friends, who would never have such an experience. Plus, many of my friends had lived with the brutal, full force of the whip of racism scarring their lives daily, while I had gotten only a sting of it, a tip of the whip. Still, I believed I needed more than God if I was going to survive racism in a country that "legally" hated me before Emancipation and hated me differently since.

At the time I began my studies, it was the late '60s, early '70s, when love was in the streets, in songs and in two fingers held as a sign for peace. What I knew from my own life was that even if some white people loved me, many more white people feared black people. I had been made the Boogeyman. I am the Boogeyman still today. This is what I call one of the "consequences of fear."

When people feel insecure and fearful, these emotions yearn for a physical manifestation, a way to leave the body and show their masters that they are right to be afraid.

When the Emancipation Proclamation freed me, it wasn't the physical bodies and imaginative minds that those white people with economic power feared, it was the possibility that I might rise and be powerful too.

That I might become as powerful as them.

That they might have to share power and wealth.

And so fear said: Make these darker people into monsters roaming the earth, untethered.

This is the legacy of slavery. I must be a monster so the white man can feel superior, which he has confused with freedom. The problem is the fearful ones have to make the shift, have to realize they are suffering from fear. Have to believe that fear is unreasonable and a killer of the feared as well as those who fear. Have to believe that love is a powerful anecdote to everything.

There is no way for me to tell this story without using the old vernacular of "the white man" and "the black man," though I don't view the world in this way. There are many times when I think the English language is inadequate, that perhaps any language that comes from our minds and thoughts, is inadequate. I am certain God has a much greater palette of words and thoughts. But right now, I am here, in this place.

When I speak of "white," I am speaking of Eurocentric thought, not of a white person.

We in the United States live in an ego-based society, designed by white men who wanted to protect and keep in their control everything ego-related, mainly physical wealth and all expressions of it. A true egoist cannot afford to love or respect a living, breathing commodity such as a slave. Opening up to love is a slippery slope that could end in the shifting of perceptions and the deterioration of the lynchpin of fear that supports an ego-based society.

It is much easier to explain the reasons you should withhold pure love from a slave, when an entire twisted system of laws and rules have been constructed to support this withholding and, ultimately, to nurture the fears of those who designed the system. But once the living, breathing commodities are free and others can see that the lines of definition between them and the slaves are blurred, there is the possibility that love, being as powerful as it is, will covet what was once unapproachable. Pure love is like water, always seeking to flow. So a new system had to be constructed. I was given oversized lips, a big butt, uncontrollable sexual urges and the omnipresent head rag, while my man was given the strength, sexual desire, and mentality of a beast.

And this is where we are today.

Not yesterday. Today.

I am convinced that what the white man fears most is death. I am not just speaking of physical death, though that kind of physical disappearance is the looming reason for all fears. In other words, other forms of death are birthed from this greatest fear.

Losing power is equivalent to death to the white founders of these United States and their lineage. Even if they don't know this consciously, it is what they believe. Their ego says, "What we own is more important than anything else." And they may think they own a country, a financial system, an economy. In fact, they believe that they *are* what they own. And they are against anything that threatens this, though really there is no threat or nothing to fear except in their consciousness that has made them a prisoner to fear.

Fear in the form of loss of power, a.k.a. death of the ego, is what made Gov. George Wallace stand in the doorway at the University of Alabama in 1963 to stop two black students from attending. Fear shape-shifted into a Remington rifle that fatally shot Martin Luther King. More recently, this type of fear made Donald Trump say Barack Obama was not born in the United States.

Fear incarcerates over two million people in the United States, half of whom are black. We hire police officers to protect us from those we fear, which is like saying there are bullseyes on the backs of every black man and woman, the beastly monsters who have been wild since being freed from slavery.

To confuse us, fear takes on a different nature the longer it is sustained, because it was not meant to be sustained at one level for a long period of time—for decades or centuries. It is a chameleon that disguises itself so you don't even recognize it is fear. The belief that there are not enough resources in the world to share with others comes from fear. The belief that another group of people is responsible for the loss of jobs doomed by technology comes from fear.

Slavery did not invent fear, but it gave people a system of thinking that supported it, legally.

Fear is meant to be a warning, part of a survival instinct. In the wild, we fear something and we make an adjustment. We sense the fear without seeing it. But what is murderous today is this sustained fear that men have created; this fear held up by a platform of rhetoric and usually spit out to increase or save profit; fear deliberately sustained to allow some people to hold on to the power they fear losing because losing power is equal to death for the ego-centered powermonger.

This fear aims to kill me, a black person, first, or to have me killed by a Zimmer-man who thinks he has been ordered to kill me because I am the descendant of slavery. But this fear is also aimed at new people at different times.

Who have the huge egos decided we should fear now? Muslims? Transgender people? People who are formerly incarcerated? Members of the Black Lives Matter movement?

It is to the advantage of the big egos to have us fear one another. They have always used fear as a weapon of control. Fear your neighbor, especially if your neighbor is black. Fear the Muslim, who is a terrorist who will kill you. Fear transgender people because they are abominations not possibly made by God and will ruin your relationship with Him.

You are not your brother's keeper. This notion of loving your neighbor cannot exist in a fearful world.

So we arrive in this space and place in time, 2017, when we see our greatest manifestations of fear besides war: prisons. This is where every lower thought white men have had converges to manifest in another brutal system that creates physical bars and locks and fences. Prisons are the long shadow of slavery cast on the earth of today.

One day, when historians look back at us, they will say: "They locked up millions of human beings in prisons." And they will cluck their tongues because, with their zoom perspective they will know that locking up humans does not reduce fear or make anyone safer. We have become people who can see only with our eyes. We have forgotten the real reason for fear, and thus we have lost much of spiritual power. We have weakened our spiritual abilities with distractions deliberately created by people who want us to focus on fear.

We see with our eyes—not with the love in our hearts—and so we see people who will hurt or kill us, take our jobs, change our institution of marriage. We build walls and prisons to separate ourselves from them and from our own fears.

But prisons and walls are the physical confirmations that the cycle of fear will continue. And they block us from the truth: we imprison whom we fear, whom those white, ego-based powermongers have pointed their fingers at—the poor, the black and brown people, the people they believe will cause them to lose their wealth. For them, it is so much easier to count slaves and prisoners than it is to change.

Thoughts become material with continual support in the form of consistent energy. Since slavery, we have put a lot of energy into these beliefs that identify whom and what we should fear.

Yet the perpetual optimist in me teaches that all of this can shift when love overtakes fear.

Of course, there are people who fear this, too. Some of us who are not wealthy or white and therefore are seen as powerless have become so used to fear that we do not recognize it. We wear it comfortably, though it is an old and heavy overcoat that drags us down. Fear is all some of us know, and therefore we do not want to relinquish it, will feel naked without it.

When slavery was openly practiced, and wealth was worshipped as much as, if not more than God, the Emancipation Proclamation was a temporary respite, and enslavement was reclaimed by white men who freed our bodies but made us someone you should fear.

We don't have video of the horror. But I know what the scream of a baby being torn from his mother sounds like. The idea of that happening over and over as families were torn apart resonates in my soul; how many years I will dream that those bodies at the bottom of the Atlantic could have saved Africa from the rampant fear that has consumed much of it; how long I will feel ungrounded because my spirit knows its home, but my body can't feel it—and so I am consumed by a restlessness no doctor has named or can cure.

What will save me, will save us all, and begin the healing from our history is if you look at me and see love. What is best for me is that I am not used to mirror your fears but instead, the slate is wiped clear so I can see my own reflection.

FORGED BY FIRE

Tim Reid

Of the many things that remain heinous about Slavery in America is how often people want to bury it, to force black Americans to forget it, to tamp it down like it never happened.

But Slavery is like Cancer. So to help anyone who thinks that black people should just move on, perhaps I can explain using that absolute analogy.

To be told that you have Cancer is one of the most life-shattering statements that any human could ever hear. In my case, the doctor's tone, although he had delivered the message many times, held a measure of compassion. I went numb as the words infiltrated my mind. I tried to make sense of them.

A sudden burst of air entered my body, signaling that I had momentarily stopped breathing. . . . I have prostate Cancer?

All I could think was that this "thing" had invaded my body, hiding out in my prostate with but one purpose, to take me out. I began to wonder, "How . . . ? What had I done to warrant such a fate?" Guilt's agenda seems to always lurk in the dark recesses of one's mind, ready to butt in at any opportune moment.

In the midst of dark wonder, the strangest thoughts can take charge of the mind. For me, it was the story of Job that took center stage. I remembered a pact I made with myself after reading the story of Job in the Bible; whereupon I declared that whatever misfortune life had in store for me, I would not utter the words of Job: "Why me, God?"

No matter how hard I tried to imprison the question, it began to bubble up from the recesses of my ego. Poised with all the sanctimony I could muster—which at the time wasn't much, I might add—I mumbled softly, "Why me, God?"

A bittersweet smile formed on my face as I remembered God's answer to Job: "Why not you . . . who are you that you should not suffer?" Well, that kind of reasoning certainly brings one closer to reality. "But I'm special," doesn't carry much weight when you are questioning God. Besides, right about now, pissing off the Big Guy isn't the best move.

Cancer is an imposing, ugly bully that comes into your life to dominate and challenge every fiber of your being. There's no hiding from this intruder; you surrender and allow this beast its appointed conclusion, or you fight with all the power you can muster.

That description sounds exactly like what I've read and heard for years about Slavery. Slavery didn't just happen. Slavery existed. It was, and is. My ancestors survived it or they didn't. But the pain of it never leaves you. You live with the scars of enduring it. You live with the constant reminders that it was a part of your family's life.

You live with the memories of those who didn't survive it—the tragic and heartbreaking reminders of what might have been and paths that diverged from life, liberty and happiness.

You live with the fear that it could take over your life or take power over your life again—a brutal overseer that commands what you eat, how you live and whether you have the strength to love the way you once did.

Slavery is like Cancer, a condition that doesn't go away but lives in the stories of your grandparents or the discrimination that hollowed out the lives of your parents and others through a century of society trying to maintain it covertly.

It isn't covert to me, to us, to ours.

And living Slavery, like living with Cancer, means constantly searching for ways to make sure you are not enslaved. It means living in fear.

With actual Cancer, first come the words.

Then Fear becomes the first opponent tossed into your new reality, as fate urgently demands that you face your mortality. All things that were important before Cancer's introduction instantly lose meaning and purpose. That very thing you've spent your life avoiding now looms larger than life itself.

Death enters stage right and demands respect.

My nature is to fight when threatened. In years past, there were times it would have been wiser to retreat from battle, but, like I said, it's not my nature.

I wondered about all the people who had heard those words before me, and all those people who did not have the means that I did to gear up.

I geared up.

Regardless of my yesterdays, I was now locked in the "mother of all battles." The quest to live and love as long as humanly possible never had greater meaning than at the moment I was told I had Cancer.

I didn't call out to the ancestors for strength, though theirs was a strength that could survive anything. I called out to the progeny to come, those who will carry forth all that we do now.

I thanked them for the support of family and friends in the present, who became my weapons to begin the hard work to fashion a survival plan. Luckily, with my Cancer, the cure rate is better than average. I started with those odds, but I knew, from that day forward, that life would never be quite the same.

I kept my spirit as close to peace as life would allow and prayed that God would grant me the courage to forge a good fight and withstand the molten fires of doubt.

I stood fast, knowing that my freedom to keep creating, keep smiling, keep loving my beloved family depended on that fight.

I imagined that fight to pursue happiness in the many places where the ancestors were forged by fire. The will to survive horrific bondage means you cannot afford to give in to powerlessness. Fighting Cancer means you cannot give in to powerlessness.

That spirit, held up by my great-grandparents, grandparents, parents, wife, remains, always. Like my ancestors, my family, my friends, we will always fight enslavement. For me, I will not be enslaved by Fear, by Cancer.

And I pray that, upon meeting the Grim Reaper, I will not cower at his command to follow, but will simply say—as so many before me did—"Not yet."

ETERNAL BONDAGE

Leonard Pitts Jr.

The shackles are the first things you see.

They are filmed in lingering close-up as the opening credits roll, a montage of them manacling the wrists, ankles, necks, and dreams of African American men. First, you see slave chains. Then, you see handcuffs. The images intermingle until, after a moment, it is hard to tell—or remember—the difference.

So begins *Get on the Bus*, Spike Lee's often overlooked near-masterpiece from 1996 about a group of African American men on a chartered ride cross-country to join the Million Man March. The movie, like the march it celebrates, represented an end-of-century accounting of where African American men stood, a statement of rivers crossed and mountains climbed, and of rivers and mountains yet to go.

As such, it is appropriate that the film begins with shackles and cuffs. Lee has seldom been accused of subtlety, and the metaphor—the criminal injustice system is the new slavery—might feel strikingly obvious.

Nevertheless, something about it tightens the line of your jaw and drives a barb into your heart. You realize that while the metaphor might indeed be striking in its obviousness, it is also striking in its truth.

From slavery to sort of freedom, America's primary goal where people of African descent are concerned has always been painfully apparent: to control an inconvenient population. That is the through-line from slavery's origins in the 17th century to its echoes here in the 21st: an imperative to regulate, manage, and constrain every aspect of black life. And that imperative only became more pronounced once the 13th Amendment ended the practice of buying and selling people.

While slavery existed, the control of black bodies was a relatively simple matter. Both law and custom virtually bristled with mechanisms designed to allow white people to regulate black ones. From the shackles to the whips to the denial of education to the traveling passes to the Supreme Court decision declaring that a black man "had no rights which the white man was bound to respect," the machinery of slavery was calibrated to provide white people the ability to regulate black bodies.

After slavery was abolished, however, white Americans were left no ready tools for the physical control of black ones. It was to fill this void that the justice system was scrapped and an injustice system pressed into service.

It began with the Black Codes, a series of statutes passed in the former states of the Confederacy to restrict the movement and freedom of purportedly free black men and women. The Black Codes required that African Americans be able to show proof of employment under penalty of arrest. They provided for the beating or forced labor of an African American who broke a labor contract, no matter how unfair or coercive the contract might have been. They forced African American children whose parents were deemed unable to care for them into unpaid labor for white planters.

But it wasn't simply that laws were shaped to regulate African American lives; the *enforcement* of laws became outrageously selective, effectively freeing white people to take whatever actions they deemed necessary to keep black ones in their places without fear of being held to account.

This laissez-faire attitude was what empowered the epoch of lynch law that stretched from the late 1800s to well after the Second World War. At its height, African Americans were slaughtered by mob violence at a rate of nearly one every two days. Nor were these atrocities limited to the former Confederacy; the violence also showed up in such far-flung outposts as Marion, Ind., and Yreka, Calif. The lynchings were distinguished both by their barbarism (one mob skinned a man's face, another lynched a man's dog, another slashed open a woman's pregnant abdomen) and by their explicitly public nature (advance notices were placed in newspapers, excursion trains were chartered, photographs were taken as souvenirs).

Yet the injustice system watched it all with supine indifference. The same sheriffs who were arresting black men and women for standing on sidewalks, the same prosecutors who were locking those men and women behind bars, looked the other way as these violent bacchanals unfolded.

When Abram Smith and Thomas Shipp were lynched in 1930, for instance, a photographer snapped a photo that shows the two men hanging freshly dead from a tree and a mob of white people milling about below. Despite this rather conclusive evidence, the killings were officially chalked up to "persons unknown."

But the criminal injustice system was also complicit in other ways. Consider the convict leasing system. As recounted in reporter Douglas Blackmon's Pulitzer Prize–winning book, *Slavery by Another Name*, it worked as follows:

A white businessman puts in an order with a local sheriff. He needs, say, 30 workers for his turpentine farm. So the sheriff goes out and arrests 30 black men. The charges don't matter. Some are petty—vagrancy, for instance. Some are outright false, such as falsely claiming that the black man owes a white man money.

But again, the charges are immaterial. A compliant court quickly finds the black man guilty and levies a fine—$35, let's say. That's far more than an indigent black man can pay, so the white businessman who put in the order steps in and pays the court. For a fraction of what a prime male field hand would have cost in the antebellum years, that white man now has, in effect, a slave, a man who has been handed over to him by the law for a period of, say, ten months and is required to do any labor the white man requires.

Moreover, since his investment is so minimal, the white man has little incentive to provide humane care or conditions for his charge. Black men's lives were literally cheap, so their "owners" thought little of chaining them up in swamps and workhouses, feeding them gruel, working and beating them to death. In terms of treatment, in fact, the convict leasing system was actually crueler than slavery. It was often the case that a black man did not survive the grueling ordeal.

One man who did survive was released and walked away. Whereupon he was promptly re-arrested. The new charge? "Stealing" the prison clothes on his back.

Take that as evidence of how thin was the pretense that any of this had to do with law and order. No, like lynch law and the Black Codes, it was about the control and exploitation of black bodies. Blackmon reports that this system swept in hundreds of thousands of African American men in Alabama alone. And the system was in place until well after the Second World War.

All of which casts our present-day debate over the so-called war on drugs in a somewhat different light.

It is, after all, common for even those who acknowledge the racial unfairness of that war to regard it in a kind of intellectual isolation, unmoored from historical context. That is, we tend to see it mostly as a present-day reflection of America's inability to rid itself of racism.

It is, of course, that. But in a sense, that is the least of it. Because, properly understood, the war on drugs is but the latest iteration of the war for control of black bodies that has been raging since before the founding of the Republic. It is the convict leasing system reheated, the Black Codes in new clothes, and, yes, slavery by another name.

And no one can credibly argue that this was accidental.

In a 1994 interview for Harper's Magazine that was published in 2015, John Ehrlichman, chief domestic counselor to President Richard M. Nixon, described the genesis of the drug war:

"The Nixon campaign in 1968, and the Nixon White House after that, had two enemies: the antiwar left and black people. You understand what I'm saying? We knew we couldn't make it illegal to be either against the war or black, but by getting the public to associate the hippies with marijuana and blacks with heroin, and then criminalizing both heavily, we could disrupt those communities. We could arrest their leaders, raid their homes, break up their meetings, and vilify them night after night on the evening news. Did we know we were lying about the drugs? Of course we did."

In fairness, it must be noted that the Ehrlichman quote has been disputed by his family and former colleagues who say it doesn't sound like the man they know (Ehrlichman died in 1999). But the racial dimension of the drug war is also attested to by another of the president's men, H. R. (Bob) Haldeman, the chief of staff who quoted his boss as saying: "You have to face the fact that the whole problem is really the blacks. The key is to devise a system that recognizes this while not appearing to."

The argument for intentionality doesn't rest entirely on the confession of aides to a long-dead president.

No, the most effective argument for that is the sheer disproportionate impact this policy has had on the African American community. It is not too much to say that the so-called war on drugs gutted that community, placing one in four African American men under the control of the injustice system, a rate higher than any other American demographic. Nor was this a bug in the system; rather, it was a feature. A person caught with crack cocaine, a cheap form of the drug favored by African American users, faced a stiffer sentence than those caught with powdered cocaine, a more expensive form favored by white users. It took a hundred times as much powdered cocaine to get the same sentence as someone caught with crack.

Small wonder that, while white Americans are far away the biggest users and sellers of drugs, African Americans represent the largest population of those doing time for drug crimes. African Americans account for about 15 percent of drug use in this country, yet in some jurisdictions they represent 70 or 80 percent of those incarcerated for drug crimes. A 2000 study co-sponsored by the Justice Department reported that an African American drug defendant is 48 times likelier to be jailed for the crime than a white one with the same record.

Moreover, as Michelle Alexander noted in her seminal 2010 work, *The New Jim Crow*, punishment for drug crimes does not end when incarceration does. To the contrary, a drug defendant can be legally denied loans, housing, employment, and the right to vote. Given the disparity with which African Americans are funneled into the system, she concludes that these restrictions amount to nothing less than a de facto racial caste system that, in many aspects, resembles the one dismantled by the civil rights movement of the 1960s.

And it is worth noting that even at this ruinous cost to African American lives, the so-called war has been a stunning failure. Over a trillion dollars spent, over 40 million arrests made, the "land of the free" becomes the biggest jailer on the planet, and yet drug use in the first four decades after the program began rose—*rose!*—by over 2,800 percent.

So we here we stand, 150 years after slavery putatively ended, 150 years into a campaign to restore by the judiciary what armies took away. Spike Lee nods to this, too, in *Get on the Bus*. As shackles are the first things you see, they are also the last.

You are in the Lincoln Memorial and the camera pans down from the white marble figure of the 16th president. A gospel organ swells in a crescendo and there they are, lying at Lincoln's feet, the shackles open and abandoned, the men long gone. It feels less like a statement of freedom than of the enduring hope thereof. Because a century and a half after Appomattox, a system of criminal injustice continues to manacle the limbs and dreams of African American people—and much of the nation looks at this and calls it freedom.

So, yes, there are rivers and mountains yet to go.

SPORTS INDUSTRIES
AS PLANTATIONS
Kevin B. Blackistone

In the wake of a loss in the long grind of a recent National Basketball Association season, Andre Iguodala, a black player (as are most in the league) was asked about a strategy of his coach, Steve Kerr—who is white, like most coaches in the league.

"No clue," Iguodala said.

Then, recalling our collective imagination of how a slave might respond when summoned, Iguodala feigned subservience: "I do what master say."

The N.B.A. fined Iguodala $10,000. It deemed its player's comment racially insensitive.

But Iguodala's allusion to the relationship between black male bodies and those who lord over the multibillion-dollar enterprise that is the athletic industrial complex was not wide of the mark.

As I noted in an entry to the Oxford African American Studies Center, when Virginia passed a law in 1705 permitting landowners to list slaves as property, the slaves who trained horses were among the first cataloged. And those slaves who trained horses became the predominant riders who raced horses in the 19th century and, as such, the first black Americans identified as athletic competitors.

There was a reason the first Kentucky Derby, in 1875, was won by a black jockey aboard Aristides. He was Oliver Lewis, a 19-year-old born in Fayette County, Kentucky. Thirteen of the fifteen jockeys in that race were black. Black jockeys, most borne of stable workers, groomers, and trainers, won 11 of the first 15 Derbies.

So there is more history than hyperbole when linking plantation exploitation to modern-day sporting life and when it comes, in particular, to black males.

The development of black male athleticism, whether in North America or elsewhere, as scholars Paul Darby, Gerard Akindes, and Matthew Kirwin argued in a 2007 article on African soccer players in European leagues, can be "interpreted as a form of neocolonial exploitation in that it involves the sourcing, refinement, and export of raw materials, in this case African football talent, for consumption and wealth generation in the European core."

Indeed, the first stop in the trans-Atlantic trade was the island of Hispaniola, which Spanish and French colonialists infamously invaded and divided into the nations of the Dominican Republic and Haiti, respectively. The former has become the top exporter of Latin American human capital to Major League Baseball.

The terms of the trade, however, have always tipped in favor of professional baseball, which buys Dominican teenage talent by the bushel and in recent years incubated it in what the game calls baseball academies. I call them farms to develop crops of boys of color, most plucked from families that make up the third of the Dominican Republic that subsists in poverty. Like the enslaved Africans who were deposited on Hispaniola, they have little to no choice about for whom they will ply their trade.

A study by the economics scholar Carrie A. Meyer found that the salaries earned by Dominican ballplayers didn't result in any economic transformation for their country. Instead, the system is reflective of the plantation capitalism analysis of sport offered by Darby, Akindes, and Kirwin.

The inability of athletic talent of color to share more equitably in the profits it produces, and where it produces it, ties together the experiences of athletes of color, no matter the economics of the arena. To be sure, there is no corner of sports in which the plantation critique is more appropriate than in the unique so-called amateur confines of college sports, where the labor force that produces most of the wealth—predominately black males—is vastly undercompensated. And those who control it—mostly white men—are largely enriched.

A study by the researcher Shaun Harper found that black males made up less than 3 percent of all undergraduate students but more than half of the football and basketball teams that are the revenue-generating college sports, estimated to be worth as much as $13 billion. While compensation for those athletes from that revenue is largely restricted to tuition, room and board, and the promise of a college education—which is questionable given that they graduate at lower rates than any other group of students—those who coach them and control their lives on college campuses are allowed to share those profits without constraint. The average annual salary for head football and basketball coaches in the five major college athletic conferences ranged between $2.8 million and $3.2 million.

And those salaries, as well as the cost of financing college sports that black males don't play—like golf, crew, and swimming and diving, as well as women's sports—are, nonetheless, paid for by the blood and sweat of black males, not unlike the plantation economy that was fortified by the labor of their forefathers, and -mothers, in the fields.

Some observers have argued that it is unfair—disrespectful even to slaves—to compare the conditions of black athletes, remunerated with potentially debt-free college educations, or million-dollar pro sports contracts, to the horrific plight of human chattel.

But the comparison isn't about human suffering. It is about a similar discordant arrangement of power, wealth and labor in which the athletic progeny of enslaved Africans find themselves.

The bondage, even self-assumed, is still bondage.

WHAT SLAVERY MEANS TO ME
Betty DeRamus

I was eight years old the day I wandered into a whites-only ice cream shop and ordered vanilla ice cream. I'll never forget standing in that shop while the man behind the counter, a man with ham-sized hands, battered me with questions.

"Who are you? And where on earth are you from?"

Eventually, the man served me, a little brown girl from Detroit, but his words—not the friendly banter of a soda jerk or bartender, but interrogation of someone in the wrong place—stayed with me.

And that encounter, in a small Alabama town whose name I don't remember, changed my life.

It was the day my relatives had to begin explaining the dangers of 1950s-era Alabama.

I had to learn the rules.

I never again entered any store anywhere without taking the temperature of the place. Would I be followed? Would I be ignored?

Yeah, I know, a black man has occupied the White House, been leader of the free world. But remember those ugly emails about the White House lawn becoming a watermelon patch?

White Americans claimed that they enslaved black Africans because we were just childlike heathens born to sweat and serve. The smell of such beliefs still hangs in the air centuries later.

I've smelled that stench my entire life.

When I was attending a mostly white high school, a teacher urged me to attend business school instead of pursuing a college degree in English. Fortunately, I ignored her.

When I was attending Wayne State University in the 1960s, a humanities professor made me retake an exam because he couldn't believe that his only black student had turned in a perfect paper.

When I was in my twenties, a friend and I once stopped at a roadside store while traveling through a rural patch of Michigan. Before buying a candy bar, I read all the labels, hoping to find something relatively healthy. The store owner kept pushing me to purchase something. Finally, he telephoned somebody and held a whispered conversation. Soon, a pickup truck parked outside the store, the driver's shotgun visible through the window. Did that store owner really think my friend and I had journeyed hundreds of miles to rob a ratty little store full of stale candy bars?

Yeah, it's still in the air—the suspicions, the fears, the doors that look open but remain closed.

Slavery followed me through my childhood, and it follows me to this day.

IF AMERICA HAD BELIEVED THAT BLACK GIRLS WERE GIRLS

Tamara Winfrey-Harris

I cannot think about slavery without thinking about the children.

Children are the physical embodiment of hope and possibility. They are blank slates. We nurture their curiosity and ambition. They can be anything. We want them to be great.

Children are innocent. We protect them. We approach them with gentle hands and words. We shield them from difficult things.

Children are *children*. We allow them their growing bodies and developing brains and the missteps and faulty judgments of youth. We give them chances.

There were no children among the enslaved in antebellum America.

Yes, there were black baby boys and growing adolescent girls. But there were no blank slates. Black people were labeled from birth by the lies slavers told to absolve their own sins. There was no innocence that needed to be preserved, nurtured, and cared for, only work to be done and hard, adult lessons to be learned. There was no forgiveness for the folly of youth. Black mistakes, no matter how young the perpetrator, always merited exacting punishment.

There were no children among the enslaved in antebellum America, just property that had not yet come into its full usefulness. What people who believe that slavery ended in 1865 do not understand is that the mind-set created by that atrocity lives now.

The racism that was an integral feature of American slavery robbed black girls and boys of their childhoods. And as I weigh the experiences of modern black girls in the United States, I am forced to ask: what has changed? They are rarely presumed innocent, treated gingerly, or given the benefit of the doubt outside black homes and communities (and sometimes not even there). In 2017, black girls still cannot be children.

In the fall of 2015, a student at Spring Valley High School in Columbia, S.C., captured video of a white male sheriff's deputy grabbing a teenage black girl by her neck, flipping her at her desk and dragging her across the room. The girl had been insolent (in other words, a teenager), refusing to give up the phone she had been using to text rather than pay attention in class. She was handcuffed and arrested, along with another black girl who attempted to defend her. The video went viral and caused a national uproar.

Teenage surliness does not merit police brutality, certainly not in a space where children are sent to be nurtured and educated. Even as the Richland County sheriff acknowledged that his deputy's actions were ill-advised, he said the student "bears some responsibility" for her assault. And at a school board meeting, a white parent assured the room: "This is not a race issue. This is, 'I want to be defiant and not do what I'm told.'" Other skeptics insisted the black girl must have done something, something that wasn't captured by video, to have earned such rough and risky treatment.

Black mistakes, no matter how young the perpetrator, always merit exacting punishment.

The Spring Valley assault was not the first incidence of brutality against a black girl to make headlines that year. In January 2015, enraged white homeowners in a subdivision in McKinney, Texas, called the police when black teens and others gathered at the neighborhood pool for a party. In the resulting chaos, an armed police officer dragged a fifteen-year-old black girl to the ground by her hair and straddled her small, brown, bikini-clad body, pressing his knees into her back. In a video of that incident, the girl can be seen begging for her mother.

The next year, in Chicago, a six-year-old black girl with special needs was placed in handcuffs by a resource officer and sent to sit near her elementary school's boilers for an hour. According to some of her classmates, the girl had stolen a piece of candy from the teacher's desk. "I'm teaching her a fucking lesson," the officer reportedly said.

It is unfathomable that a white American girl, even a defiant one, would ever be treated this way—choked, dragged, pinned under a grown man while barely clothed, banished to a schoolhouse boiler room. It is even harder to believe society would find it conscionable. During the 2016 presidential election, Republican leaders remained unmoved by their nominee's jingoism and racism, which stood to harm black Americans, including a great many girls. But when Donald J. Trump bragged about (white) pussy-grabbing, G.O.P. leaders wavered, invoking their darling daughters. America has historically viewed white women and girls as delicate, virginal, and in need of protection.

Meanwhile, justification for the mistreatment of black girls often hinges on slavery-era stereotypes about black girls and traditions on how to treat them—even if those stereotypes exist only subconsciously in the minds of perpetrators. For instance, enslaved black women and girls were masculinized, positioned as diametric opposites to white, middle-class women and girls, to excuse often brutal workloads. That early characterization of the bestial black woman continues to affect the ways black girls are seen and treated in American society. Those officers in South Carolina and Texas and Chicago were simply treating black girls as they have long been treated: as men, and *black* men specifically—unnaturally strong, aggressive and dangerous. Not children, but threats to be neutralized.

In antebellum America, enslaved black women were also sexualized to excuse the naked probing of the auction block, routine sexual assaults and the use of black female bodies to breed new human property. Masters could not be guilty of forcing themselves on women in bondage if those women were libidinous and un-rape-able. This is another lie that has chased black women and girls over centuries, a distortion used today to justify treating little girls like sexually mature sirens.

For instance, black girls are disproportionately targeted by sexist school dress code violations that police girls' clothing in order to assuage the allegedly rampaging and uncontrollable libidos of male teachers and students.

But there is much worse.

The group Black Women's Blueprint estimates that 60 percent of black girls will have experienced sexual assault by the time they reach age eighteen—a stunning statistic made more sickening by the knowledge that for every black woman or girl who reports her rape, at least fifteen will remain silent. And for black women and girls who do come forward about being assaulted, the influence of the centuries-old black Jezebel myth means they may not be believed or receive assistance. A study published in the *Psychology of Women Quarterly* in 2017 revealed that white female college students are less likely to help their black peers who are at risk of rape.

There is no innocence that needs to be preserved, nurtured, and cared for.

Black female bodies are still read as invitations—even, sadly, within black communities. A black professor recalled on Facebook how her elders once monitored her pubescent body: "Jiggling booties were horrifying to my mama and her mama. They were both small-breasted and worried that my triple-D-by-high-school breasts would draw unwanted attention or meant that I was already sexually active."

The sometimes paralyzing ways mamas and grandmamas fret over black girls' bodies and the language used to discuss developing black girls (fast-tail, ho) in real life and popular culture reinforce the idea that every black girl is a budding Jezebel. So, too, does the cover the black community often gives adult male abusers of black girls. In

2004, as R&B performer R. Kelly awaited trial for allegedly having sex with an underage black girl, the NAACP nominated him for its iconic Image Award.

Black people are labeled from birth by the lies slavers told to absolve their own sins. And sometimes, over time, black folks start believing those lies.

Children are the physical embodiment of hope and possibility.

Children are innocent.

Children are *children*.

Black girls, though, are criminalized and sexualized.

This should be America's great shame: a white man with a badge in 2017 can look at a black girl, assess her through the same biases as a white man in 1817 and treat her no differently from her enslaved ancestors. Most girls in the black community will know the pain of sexual assault before they are even eighteen. And in their own communities, black girls' spreading hips and budding breasts are believed to give license for exploitation. It is indefensible. A damned abomination.

America, a country that gives loud voice to its supposed love and care for future generations, tells on itself each time a black girl is mistreated—dragged, banished, or objectified—and the majority say nothing or, perhaps worse, twist the mistreatment into evidence of that child's deficiency.

This country cannot be said to have moved past its slaving past until *black* children are the physical embodiment of hope and possibility, until *black* children are innocent, until *black* children are children.

Until then, none of us is free.

KALIEF BROWDER

A LIFE MARKED FOR DEATH

Vann R. Newkirk II

The noose was fitted from birth.

This one, the power cord of an air conditioning unit. Plastic and wires replaced the hard hemp knot, but the end result still the same. A dead black body; a spirit extinguished. At once, a tethering and an untethering, a joining of a broken soul with a broken form. In this instance, the tying hands were his own, but they'd been guided by others'; they'd given him a rope and a tree and set a fire under his feet. And like the sundered people who'd begat those who'd begat those who'd begat those who tried to protect him from the very same system that destroyed generations, the only real choice was to die from the fall or live as a ghost.

Kalief Browder's death wasn't a suicide; rather, it was a murder committed by a hand that stretched from plantation to prison.

Two years in solitary confinement will destroy any man. It will crumble the soul from the outside in, until all that's left is the raw nerve of pain. A cruel but all-too-usual punishment, in a cruel but all-too-usual system. An instrument of torture in a corrupt and topsy-turvy world of torture, a world where prison beds are projected and reserved for black boys at the first sign of distress. It is a system of punishment, designed with the end goal of brutal efficiency: of creating prisons out of the fabrics of our own lives.

Kalief entered that torture chamber at 16, the age when white peers are given litanies of chances to fail, learn, and grow. Born in the Bronx and raised under his mother's watchful eye, Kalief was sent as a teenager to Rikers, an island of pain operating in spite of numerous documented violations of the basic tenets of humanity. He spent three years enduring recorded beatings by guards and inmates, long periods of solitary confinement, and failed suicide attempts. His stay had been extended simply because his family could not afford bail.

The charge that sent him to that bastion of brutality? An alleged theft of a backpack.

That charge was dropped.

Two years after Kalief was finally released from Rikers, he completed the deed that he'd tried before in prison. So ended five years of unspeakable pain, inflicted by the hands of a thoroughly corrupt, brutal, and inadequate policing, prosecution, and incarceration complex that manages—without irony—to somehow still be referred to as a justice system. That system killed him. That system gave him his noose and told him to jump. It ruined a child. It ruined a family and a community. It added his name to the litany of names of black girls and boys and women and men that we recite like names from a prayer book as we march and cry out. That list has become our own perverse Deuteronomy, a canon of the numbers of those crushed under the boot heel of white supremacy. His name and the names on that list are America's blood debt, as is the red stain on the conscience of all of us who watched but did not cry out.

To act as if that canon of pain to which Kalief Browder now belongs is a new thing, a thing created in response to the cries of "Black lives matter" and "stop killing us" that ring the streets to this day, is fallacy. As W. E. B. Du Bois noted over a hundred years ago in

The Souls of Black Folk, the system of policing and mass incarceration that fashioned Browder's noose arose with that very *teleos* not as an incidental element but as a core part of its purpose.

"The police system of the South was originally designed to keep track of all Negroes, not simply criminals," Du Bois wrote. "Thus grew up a double system of justice, which erred on the white side by undue leniency . . . and erred on the black side by undue severity, injustice, and lack of discrimination." That double system acts in concert mostly with the less-sanctioned acts of white terror from those in white sheets and the free radicals, and connects Kalief to millions who came before. The bloody history of black death in America is a long one that never went away, and its official arms have been stained most.

The fact of the matter is that brutality and the double system create the permanent black underclass, as it sows the bones of young men and women like Kalief Browder to continue its harvest of death and pain. The two are one—state-sponsored and -encouraged violence *are* "the race problem" in America and always have been. Our cry is to "stop killing us," yes, but in a deeper sense, it is to stop the simultaneous cultural degradation and exile. To stop marginalizing us to the polluted edges of cities. To stop pulling the safety nets out from under us. To stop using the police as mercenary occupying forces in our neighborhood, to stop replacing every single social service occupation with patrolmen. To stop imprisoning us, to stop beating and bullying us. To stop shooting us with our hands up. To stop fashioning our nooses before we are even given our names. To end the continuum of pain that enslavement begat, and to begin the work of liberation?

Kalief Browder's death was not a suicide. It was a critical failure of humanity. We owed him then, and we owe him now, only now the debt can never be repaid.

He was twenty-two years old.

AN ABOMINATION, BUT YOU GOT FED

Julianne Malveaux

"Slavery," the man said, "was an abomination. But you got paid,
you got food, you got clothes. You got housing."

The man is sitting at my mama's table, after sharing Christmas dinner
with the Malveaux family. As folks drift out, he and his girlfriend are
the last to leave. And before they go, they treat my youngest sister,
Antoinette, and me to a bunch of crazy pro-Trump talk. They object
when I describe capitalism as "predatory," and they disavow the notion that racism is woven into our nation's roots.

Slavery is "an abomination," but one that we have "overcome," he
insists.

The entire encounter would be amusing, except the European
American man is over seventy, and he ought to know better. He
ought to know better, especially, to talk spit at the table of his African American host whose activist daughters are poised to verbally
eviscerate him. But white skin and privilege means he doesn't have

to do context. He can say what he wants, when he wants, where he wants. And walk out of the house with a shopping bag full of food.

My mom is a retired social worker, a "go to Mass as often as possible" Catholic. She used to play the organ for the choir, but age and illness have made her choir time infrequent. She still loves the choir, though, and was happy to see the racist man—I'll call him Paul—singing at midnight Mass. Spontaneously, she invited him to come eat dinner with us on Christmas Day.

That's my mom.

She invites everyone.

And because she was a social worker, we were used to seeing her bring clients home, give them our new clothes and tell us we had much to be grateful for and needed to understand and empathize with those who had less. So it was entirely in character that she would invite Paul. (Later, she would say that she did not know he felt so strongly about the 45th president, and that he was so ignorant about enslavement.) Still, she fussed at me for raising my voice and asked if I thought I'd changed the man's mind about anything.

Paul was a jerk, and a greedy jerk at that. While other folks were playing rise and fly at the dining room table, he and his girlfriend sat there for at least three hours, gorging themselves. Antoinette and I played waitress, refilling soup and salad bowls and glasses of wine. At one point we noted that Paul seemed hungrier than most. But, up to a point, we enjoyed the fact that he enjoyed our mom's hospitality. Mom enjoys a house full of people, convivial conversation and lots of laughter. Neither she nor Paul saw the irony in a man saying that slaves "got fed" and then walking out of the home of a descendant of slaves with a gallon-sized container of chowder, a big bowl of salad, bread, pie, and beverages!

What does our nation's history of enslavement have to do with that dinner or today's challenges? The conversation with Paul says it all. Too many Americans, regardless of race, ignore our nation's second "original sin." They do not understand that there would be no Capitol building and no White House without the labor of the enslaved. And no, Paul, enslaved people didn't get paid, and the food they did get was paltry.

Enslaved people got one outfit of clothing, once a year. Their housing was, at best, deficient. I'd love to take Paul, Dr. Ben Carson, the 45th president and a few more so-called leaders and lock them in the basement of the National Museum of African American History and Culture until they were visited with good sense—or force them to watch a series of films while chained to their chairs.

We could start with *Sankofa*, and go to *12 Years a Slave*, and maybe end with either the old or the new version of *Roots*. We could throw Nate Parker's *The Birth of a Nation* in there, too, so they could see the scene where an iron implement is shoved into a man's mouth as he is forced to eat. Most Americans don't know our history, and many don't want to know it. But we relive it, live with it, and couldn't escape it even if we wanted to. And we are the ones who must remind people so the heinousness of the atrocity is never forgotten.

People whose families came to this country after the Civil War, recent immigrants, often claim, "But my family did not own slaves."

So?

Your family benefited from enslavement and the never-ending aftermath of Negro exclusion from the labor market, from the land grabs, from the unions, from the favorable federal terms for grants and loans, especially in the post-World War II era. Some African Americans were able to thrive through some of these programs. Most were excluded.

Enslavement not only disadvantaged a people, it created a set of stereotypes about inferiority that were eagerly consumed by European Americans who found it easy to believe that those with darker skin were somehow less than human. This allowed, and continues to allow, the institutional racial exclusion. It set the stage for African American people to litigate and protest for basic human rights—the right to use the bathroom or the water fountain, to attend college and professional schools, to work for the government, to purchase homes.

European Americans went to absurd lengths to maintain their

illusion of superiority. In Oklahoma, for example, George McLaurin was denied the opportunity to attend graduate school at the University of Oklahoma because state law did not allow black and white students to be educated together. McLaurin sued and he was admitted, but he was provided with separate facilities: a designated table in the cafeteria, a desk in the library and a desk just outside the classroom where lectures were taking place. He sued again, and eventually was allowed to attend the university without restrictions regarding his seating, his library access, or his cafeteria interactions. How fragile must the illusion of superiority be that European Americans construct such an elaborate structure of exclusion? This happened in 1948, not yesterday, yet echoes of the McLaurin case remain when European Americans continue to intimidate or kill based on the fragility of their supposed superiority (see Dylan Roof).

Would race relations be different if more people were educated about enslavement? Would they be different if fewer were ambivalent about the Civil War and its aftermath? The Civil War was fought over slavery, with the Confederate Constitution referring to Black inferiority. The South lost (yes, lost, y'all), but many have clung to the symbols of losing with Confederate flags and statues, celebrations and memorials. So if you get on Highway 95 out of Washington, D.C., you will drive down Jefferson Davis Highway, named after the traitor who was president of the Confederacy. Depending on where you are in Maryland or Virginia (not to mention farther south), you will find a statue to some Confederate, faithfully tended by descendants of other Confederates. They say they are simply honoring their ancestors, but their ancestors were racist losers. Where are the monuments to the lynched, the maimed? And why do so many schools in the South teach the Confederacy as if it is sacred? Race relations might be different if racism were confronted forcefully and frequently. Instead, in these United States, we have a member of Congress (Iowa Republican Steve King) who openly advocates a European American hegemony.

Our nation's very foundation is racism, enslavement, predatory capitalism, and violence. Our nation's foundation is anchored on a willful ignorance, with both Presidents John Adams and Thomas Jefferson acknowledging the evils of enslavement and the fact that our nation would have to deal with this evil at some point in the future. My mom's friend Paul is as willfully ignorant as many Americans, regardless of race. By viewing enslavement as something that happened way back then, when we got fed and we got clothes, too many deny its impact on contemporary life. But every time someone like Steve King opens his mouth, he reminds us of our nation's basic roots in inequality. Every time David Duke gives a metaphoric high-five to our 45th president, we are reminded of the persistence of white-skin privilege.

Our nation's legacy of enslavement confronts us every day, in ways both aggressive and benign. I'm used to driving down Jefferson Davis Highway (although it gets on my nerves), but I'll never get comfortable with a Confederate flag, openly displayed.

And while I've been raised to observe my mama's hospitality standards, I'll never get used to a European American sitting at our table, eating our food, and telling me that slavery wasn't so bad because, after all, we got fed.

Paul, that's called protecting your investment, not being kind or charitable. Slave-owners fed their animals, too, sometimes better than slaves.

Dear Paul: You are a symbol for those who would minimize enslavement and its ugly aftermath of Jim Crow and persistent (and present) discrimination. Enslavement is relevant in contemporary life because it has shaped attitudes and perceptions, and rears its ugly head both forcefully and subtly.

It is still real.

It still matters.

OBJECT LESSONS
RE-ENCOUNTERING SLAVERY
THROUGH ROSE'S GIFT
Mark Auslander

As a teacher and museum director, I often struggle with how to convey the unimaginable horror of chattel slavery to my students and museum visitors. Statistics alone seem incapable of moving people. In our image-saturated world, graphic or cinematic representations of slave ships and plantation outrages, while necessary, increasingly seem insufficient. We have become so accustomed to mass media scenes of horror and subjection that we too easily turn our eyes away. Or simply turn the channel.

In his famous eulogy for the victims of the 9/11 terrorist attacks, Rabbi Marc Gellman stated (at a time when it was incorrectly believed that six thousand people had perished at the World Trade Center, at the Pentagon and on United Flight 93): "On that day six thousand people did not die. On that day one person died, six thousand times."

That simple, profound restatement compels us, in the most visceral way possible, to face directly the irreducible humanity of each and every victim of injustice. How, I have often wondered, can that startling sense of moral immediacy be conveyed in the vast shadows of the slave trade and of the slavery system, shadows that continue to haunt us to this day?

At its heart, the question facing us is how do we teach and promote empathy at a historical moment when waves of intolerance and ethnic nationalism are once more sweeping the globe? How do we come to see the self in the other, to resist the urge to turn our eyes away from the suffering of our fellow human beings, past and present? How, in effect, do we relocate ourselves into the predicament of a person who is not, at first glance, linked to us in any way?

Child psychologists tell us that children learn the vital capacity for empathy, in part, through engaging with physical objects. A toddler's blanket, doll, or teddy bear hovers ambiguously between the child's inner psychic universe and external objective reality. Under conditions of healthy development, these "transitional objects," as the great psychoanalyst D.W. Winnicott termed them, allow the child to glimpse, gradually and in fits and starts, what it really might be like to inhabit another's skin, to experience pleasure and pain within another person's life horizons. A single inanimate physical thing, paradoxically, can help a child understand the suffering and joys, the singular humanity, of other living beings.

So let's explore how a single physical thing might come to function as a "transitional object" for a nation that remains, in so many ways, in deep denial about its own childhood. We so often risk forgetting our nation's founding, original sin—the vast collective crime of enslavement, the casual buying and selling of human beings, and the shattering of untold thousands of families in the pursuit of vast financial profit.

In 2007, at a flea market in Tennessee, a white woman purchased for $20 a seeming pile of rags, which contained, to her great surprise, an old, patched cotton bag. That bag bore on its lower face this startling inscription, in embroidery:

My great grandmother Rose
mother of Ashley gave her this sack when
she was sold at age 9 in South Carolina
it held a tattered dress 3 handfulls [sic] of
pecans a braid of Roses hair. Told her
It be filled with my Love always
she never saw her again
Ashley is my grandmother

Ruth Middleton
1921

After a period of deliberation, the woman donated the bag to Middleton Place, a historic plantation museum near Charleston, S.C. Middleton Place, in turn, has loaned the object to the nation's newest Smithsonian museum, the National Museum of African American History and Culture in Washington, D.C. Since September 2016, the bag, usually called Ashley's Sack, has been displayed in the museum's Slavery and Freedom concourse, where it directly faces the opening words of the Declaration of Independence, which intones, "We hold these truths to be self-evident, that all men are created equal." There can be no more powerful reminder of the enormous gulf between the Founders' promise and the lived reality experienced by millions of people of color in the opening decades of the Republic. It is impossible to read Ruth Middleton's embroidered story, standing in front of the very object given long ago to the nine-year-old Ashley, without being overwhelmed by a sense of immediate grief, loss, outrage. This pain knows no past tense, but is happening again and again in a present moment. Somewhere, a mother is being torn from her little girl. Somewhere, a little girl is being sold away from her mother.

WHO WERE ROSE, ASHLEY, AND RUTH?

No record of the sack exists prior to its discovery in 2007. Through archival research over the past two years, I have been able to establish that Rose and Ashley were both owned, at separate locations, by the prominent Charleston-based merchant Robert Martin Sr. (ca. 1792–1852). My theory is that Ashley was sold at some point in 1853 or 1854, as Robert Martin's widow, Serena Milbery Martin, was actively settling the estate.

Ashley's granddaughter, who embroidered the sack in 1921, was evidently born Ruth Jones in 1903 in Columbia, S.C., the daughter of two servants at the University of South Carolina. By 1918, she was orphaned and had made her way up to Philadelphia, Pa., where she was, for a time, employed as a domestic servant in the home of a wealthy, white engineer. In June 1918, Ruth married Arthur Middleton, a factory worker in Philadelphia who had been born in Camden, S.C., not far from Columbia. She gave birth to a baby girl, Dorothy Helen Middleton, six months later, so was presumably pregnant when she married. Arthur was drafted two weeks after the marriage, and spent a year in Europe in the U.S. Army; he does not appear to have ever lived with Ruth after being demobilized.

Thus, when she made the embroidery in 1921, Ruth was a single mother raising a three-year-old daughter. It seems likely that she verbally recounted the family story to the child and decided to embroider the story on the bag to give it to her daughter as a gift.

After Ruth's death from tuberculosis in 1942, her daughter, Dorothy Helen, lived in the Philadelphia area until 1988, when she died in the northern Philadelphia suburb of Wyncote. She appears to have passed away in a nursing home; staff members believe that the sack was most likely donated to Goodwill. From there its movements remain unknown, until it was found in flea market, nineteen years later.

UNDERSTANDING ROSE'S GIFT

Why does this simple, frayed object so deeply move thousands of museum visitors, across all lines of race, history, and difference? Part of the bag's power, I believe, is that it transforms the usual relationship between people and objects under conditions of enslavement.

Slave-owners and slave-sellers continually attempted to turn persons into objects, into commodities that were sold on the open market and subjected to every imaginable form of physical and mental abuse. Yet here, in Rose's gift, we have a physical object that, at a moment of almost incomprehensible tragedy, resolutely conveys the fundamental humanness of enslaved people, asserting the sacredness of the parent-child bond precisely when it is most imperiled: *It be filled with my Love always.*

The soft cotton sack itself, hurriedly presented at the dreadful moment of the slave sale, may have carried a sense of the lost mother's skin. Each thing that Rose placed inside the bag, in turn, conveys the intimate bond between mother and child. Rose's tattered dress may have carried her fragrance. The handfuls of pecans carry the memory of a mother's daily labor of feeding her child. The braid of Rose's hair perhaps evoked times when Rose braided Ashley's hair.

For many of my coastal Carolina "Lowcountry" consultants, the presence of hair suggests that the sack itself functioned as a form of spiritual power—known as conjure, mojo, or obeah—intended to protect the child long after her physical rupture from her mother. An African American woman, whom I will call Alicia, observed: "Well, hair is power, as my grandmother always said. If Miss Rose put a braid of her hair in the bag, that wasn't just a keepsake, it was so she could keep and watch little Ashley." Alicia's friend, whom I will call Rachel, concurred. "I just have the feeling in my heart that sack wasn't just for carrying things, she was doing something with it, a blessing, something sacred, the way a root-worker would, I'd say." Both women emphasized that bundles containing a collection of objects have long carried the power to heal or curse. Alicia also lay emphasis on Rose's statement: "It be filled with my Love always." She noted: "Again, that's what my grandmother would do, to turn on or wake up the bundle. She'd say something, maybe just whisper it, to make it jump like, make it light up. That sack wasn't a dead thing, you see, it almost was like a living thing, traveling with little Ashley, protecting her."

Seven decades after Rose's gift to Ashley, Ashley's granddaughter

Ruth gave her daughter, Dorothy Helen, another gift, recasting the story, long passed on orally within the family, in written form. Her skillfully composed text is worth reading carefully. The first two lines introduce Rose and Ashley, explaining their relationship to each other and their relationship to the embroiderer, and clarifying that the bag upon which the needlework is being sewn is the actual object that was given so long ago. The third line recounts a painful story of the slave sale, giving both Ashley's age and the location of the sale. The fourth and fifth lines recount the physical contents of the bag.

At the end of the fifth line, the writer shifts from standard English into the African American vernacular that Rose herself must have spoken. Instead of "She told her," Ruth writes, "Told her." The next line continues in the dialect of the remembered speaker, "It be filled with my Love always." In African American vernacular English, "be" signifies a continuous, habitual state, as in "I be working every afternoon." (I am grateful to my colleague Bobby Cummings for this linguistic insight.) In that strict sense, the word "always" might be seen as redundant or added for emphasis. Significantly, the embroiderer has left a space, a beat, between the phrase "It be filled with my Love" and the reiterative "always." We might thus read the line, in effect, as "It be filled with my Love (beat) always." We might read the word "always" as "all ways," in the sense of "in all ways." To my mind, this line enlivens the sack, making it a kind of living entity, filled with the spiritual or emotive presence of the soon-to-be absent mother for all time.

Significantly, Ruth used three colors of thread. The first five lines in brown thread, roughly speaking, expand outward, leading after a space to the climactic line in red, consisting of Rose's parting statement to her daughter, "It be filled with my Love ... always." The word "Love," at the approximate center of the piece, is the largest word in the entire work, and is offset by spaces from the words before and after it. This word, "Love," more than anything else, makes the cloth bag into a kind of body that contains within it the spirit of the artist's grandmother and great-grandmother.

The final four lines narrow inward. Line seven recounts the poignant epilogue, "She never saw her again," returning to the brown thread of the upper text. Then come the final three lines, in a green thread, clarifying the artist's relationship to Ashley and signing her name and the year. Green, the color of spring and new life, conveying that Rose's family tree, against all odds, continues to flourish.

By embroidering the story on the very object that passed from the hands of mother to daughter at the moment they were severed, Ruth brings together the names of her ancestors, along, at the end, with her own name. She has recreated, out of this valued family textile, the fabric of their female lineage. The finished sack, while a lamentation of long-ago injustice, is also a tangible family reunion, sewing together those who were torn asunder, and recreating the lines of descent that the slavery system had sought to annihilate.

GIFTED

Most gifts have afterlives. As each child learns, a gift carries with it the obligation to reciprocate with further gifts. These, in turn, spawn further gifts over time that usually bind an ever-widening circle of persons together into productive bonds of mutual obligation. Gifts and return gifts, anthropologists have learned, are the foundation of human society the world over.

Torn forever from her mother at age nine, Ashley could never reciprocate her mother's parting gift. She could never care for her aging mother, giving back directly to her parent, as children normally try to do, a token of what our parents have given us. In that sense, the spirit of the gift, which ought to bind together families through continuous expression of love, was broken. That violent severing of the bonds of love was, to be sure, among the greatest crimes of the slavery system.

Yet, in other senses, Rose's gift continued across the generations. This valued legacy, of storytelling and family love, passed through a line of black women, as the object traveled northward along the epic pathways of the Great Migration.

Now in the newest Smithsonian museum, facing the words of Thomas Jefferson's Declaration, the sack becomes a different kind of gift, calling forth further acts of return engagement from each and every person who beholds it. We are given, in the most visceral and poignant sense imaginable, an intuitive understanding of both the intimacy and enormity of slavery's injustice. As sociologist Orlando Patterson reminds us, slavery imposed a form of "social death" upon millions of people, denying them legal and economic rights to full humanity. In the sack, we behold this not as a statistical abstraction but as a living, heartbreaking truth. To paraphrase Rabbi Gellman's liturgy, it is not that thousands of children were separated from their mothers, a long time in a distant place. A little girl is torn from her mother, thousands upon thousands of times. A mother sees her flesh and blood sold away forever, again and again and again. An eloquent, dignified living woman sees her hopes, dreams, and dignity assaulted, day after day, days beyond number, across thousands of hamlets, towns, and cities.

At the same time, Rose's gift gives us even more profound gifts. In its presence, we come to behold the unconquerable power of the human spirit. We are given a breathtaking illustration of the very thing that makes us most human, our capacity to honor those whom we have lost and from that loss, to be inspired to carry forward, to forge lineage and community against all the forces arrayed against us. We cannot conquer death, but we can turn our dead into honored ancestors, who sustain us through the darkest of nights.

Through this unforgettable object and through Ruth's fading needlework, improbably surviving across 170 years, we see the Dead and Living reunited. In spite of the efforts of the slavery system to turn human beings into commodities, denying them the bonds of love and family, lines of descent endure, even across physical death and the "social death" of slavery.

The African American museum stands in the shadow of the Washington Monument, which for generations has bound together all Americans as common children of our slave-owning Founding Father. Rose's gift, made not of soaring stone but of fragile cloth, brings us into a different kind of family relationship, reminding us that we are all of us, regardless of race, color or ethnicity, bound together into the national family by a shared history of slavery and its complex legacies. We are all our mother's children. We most fully honor all our mothers when we refuse to turn our faces away from the history of injustice that shaped this nation, when we strive to remember and honor all mothers and daughters in peril, and from that common memory we resolve that a better world is, indeed, possible. Rose's gift, filled with her love always, is our shared inheritance, a tangible, miraculous promise of the beloved community that is our birthright and that ought to be, in turn, our most precious gift to our children and our posterity.

CHASING MY PAST ON A DIFFERENT MAP

Paula Williams Madison

a.k.a. Lowe Xiao Na and Nana Akosua Barnie

In 2016, I hired a Chinese Trinidadian genealogist to help me find my past. After four months, she uncovered the first document I've ever seen with my paternal grandfather's name on it.

My father was the only child of John Henry Mortimer Williams—but my dad also was the eldest child born to his mother, Sarah Agatha Elizabeth Lloyd.

My father and oldest brother are both named Elrick Mortimer Williams—Sr. and Jr. I have no idea where any of those names came from, and the sad truth is I never will. I speculate that Mortimer originally belonged to a long-deceased slave-owner.

Those discoveries were not the first. I had been searching for some time. In 2008, the year Senator Barack Obama was elected president, we had my brother's DNA study done by AfricanAncestry.com and learned that we—like 90 percent of all Jamaicans—are descended from the Akan or Ashanti people of present-day Ghana.

That same year, I visited Kumasi, Ghana, and had a private audience with Asantehene, king of the Ashanti, and he named me for his deceased mother! My Akan name is Nana Akosua Barnie, a name I treasure.

Those few facts must sustain me. That little information is all I have about my African family. That is what slavery took from me. Now I can tell you what I snatched back from slavery.

I'm living a wonderful life.

I rose to the top of my profession. I built wealth by beginning to save for retirement when I was twenty-two, a plan I hatched when I was twenty-one.

I married a remarkable man, raised a brilliant daughter—a doctor—and am charmed every day by the creativity and mindfulness of a grandson who sees the world through a filter that showed him a U.S. president who looks a lot like him.

But the Atlantic slave trade left many of us unsure of our African lineage and stripped some of my African American brothers and sisters in families across the country of their ability to rise.

I am one of the lucky ones, thanks to a memory from my mother about a man named Samuel Lowe.

Like most Black children, I grew up knowing the Black stereotype, fighting against it, living with it. I remember being a young student at a Catholic grammar school in Harlem and sitting in history class. The nun was discussing the Civil War and what it meant to the end of slavery. The few Black kids in my grammar school class all recalled having the same thought: "Why are these white kids looking at me?"

It happened again in my Catholic high school in the Bronx. We reached the point in our curriculum where we were skimming over the civil rights era and the protests led by Dr. Martin Luther King Jr. and others, and I vividly recall wondering, "Why the fuck are they looking at me?"

I didn't attract those kinds of looks when we studied the English, French, and Spanish explorations and taking of America. No one stared when we discussed the Industrial Age or the women's suffrage movement or even World War II.

What I recall is Black people not being a part of those discussions. People of the African diaspora played key roles in these histories, but we never even discussed Black people in connection with history. We were tools, belongings, irrelevant in our significance as the laborers who built much of America.

They tried to make us feel invisible. I felt angry. I felt deceived.

Apart from my own self-directed study of the history of Black people, I learned the truth about the role Blacks played in this nation's development by majoring in Black Studies at Vassar College.

I also majored in history and minored in education. Decades later I realized that my undergraduate studies as well as graduate studies in journalism all were preparing me to report the most important story of my life: my own.

Yes, slavery stole the story of my African Jamaican ancestry. I lost my father's mostly African lineage. And though I learned some of my mother's biracial lineage, including our descending from the Akan people, slavery stole any chance of locating their ancestral villages and ancestors in Africa.

But my mother, who was African Jamaican and Chinese, left a thread different from those of most of my friends. So I chose to follow that path through history to define myself and not accept the definition that slavery gave African American families over generations.

My brothers, Elrick and Howard, and I set out to find my mother's Chinese siblings and their offspring in China.

How was I able to find my Chinese family, ten thousand miles away, with only a few clues as to who my grandfather was? How was I able to connect with her siblings who hadn't even known she existed? How is that possible when I look Black, don't speak any dialect of Chinese? Ironically, it was easier to find my Chinese relatives in a country of nine million square miles with 1.3 billion people than to find my African Akan/Ashante relatives in a country of ninety-two thousand square miles and twenty-seven million people.

It's easier because slavery destroyed many of the clues and connections that could take me to my ancestral village in Africa. Just as I had started asking within my own family about my African ancestry, I did the same as I pursued by Chinese ancestry.

My first step was to ask my father's brothers and sisters to help me identify where the Chinese in Jamaica came from—and they did: it was Guangdong Province in southeastern China.

With the immeasurable help of Jeanette Kong, a Hakka Chinese Jamaican documentarian who lives in Toronto, we unearthed numerous records online about my grandfather. And because Dr. Keith Lowe, who turned out to be my cousin, co-founded the Toronto Hakka Conference, my brothers and I attended the fourth conference and made the final connections linking us to our family in China.

My successful quest to find my Chinese relatives revealed a documented lineage that extends back nearly three thousand years. My family has a legacy book called a jiapu that is a record of my family members dating back to 1006 BC. It is on display in Lowe Swee Hap, our ancestral village in Shenzhen, China.

Literate Chinese families have maintained these legacy books for millennia. They routinely captured the history of the men in a family, and women were mentioned only parenthetically as the "daughter of," "sister of," "wife of" and "mother of" because it was the history of men. It is not unlike the griots Alex Haley wrote about when he discovered his "roots" and learned of his lineage from a storyteller, who recounted the village history until he heard his ancestor's name.

When I met my mother's half-brother, my Uncle Lowe Chow Woo, I asked him if my mother could be added to the jiapu, now that the family knew of her existence. He told me that it was not tradition. I'm sure the look on my face of sadness, regret, and even defiance led him to reflect on the relevance of my request. Months later, when I returned, the family's jiapu had indeed been rewritten at my uncle's direction. There, in the history of the 150th generation, was my mother's name and the name of her mixed-race half-sister, Adassa Lowe.

Uncle Chow Woo recognized that our family's history was not traditional Chinese lineage, and so he adjusted and accounted for his sisters' birth in Jamaica, the land where their father had come to love three different women and his eight children.

His Western name was Samuel Lowe. His name given at birth was Lowe Ding Chow, written 罗定朝 in Chinese. When my grandfather boarded the ship in Hong Kong, the British ship's clerk would have asked him his name. My grandfather spoke Hakka, the dialect of the Hakka people, who today number 80 million globally. That clerk would likely have recognized only one sound in my grandfather's name and so upon hearing it, he wrote it as LOWE, adding his own selection for a first name, and so my grandfather was named Samuel Lowe.

Like thousands of laborers from Guangdong Province who toiled in the Caribbean fields in the 1800s, my Hakka Chinese grandfather began a new life when, at age 15, he boarded that ship bound for Kingston in 1905. My family believes he may have "cut cane" on a sugar plantation, an occupation indentured Chinese adopted after the British abolished slavery in 1838.

Many of the freed West Africans suffered unmerciful beatings, starvation, unspeakable abuses, and even death under slavery. No longer enslaved, many refused to work—for any amount—on the British- and U.S.-owned plantations, leaving them languishing in a foreign land. The imported, indentured Chinese and Indians moved onto the fields and into the former slaves' quarters to also face starvation and brutal treatment at the hands of the same overseers who drove the enslaved Africans. And these replacement workers were paid almost nothing and worked unforgiving hours—sometimes to death.

Many of these Chinese laborers left wives and children behind in China. The three-year indentureship contracts forbade them to bring their families. Such unfair immigration laws separated families—many never to reunite. These suddenly "bachelor" Chinese often began new families with the African Jamaican women. Eventually they worked off their contracts, and while some returned to China, many became shopkeepers, taxpayers, and almost all fathered mixed-race children.

Even today, many of these children and their children are lost to their ancestral homeland, China. Many don't know how to find their clan members and ancestral villages in China.

My grandfather's life story included an eldest daughter, my mother, Nell Vera Lowe. She endured a love-starved upbringing in Jamaica's countryside; an upbringing that included a wrenching separation from her father when she was only three years old. From that cruel and loveless childhood, my mother became a lioness mom, not a tiger mom.

The way I would describe my mother, Nell Vera Lowe Williams, is she was fierce and she was sad. Fierce because she was a half-Chinese, half-African Jamaican woman raising her three Black children in 1950s Harlem. Sad because she never fit in in Jamaica. Sad because she never fit in in Harlem. Sad because she never reached her father's ancestral homeland, China.

My mother never fit in. Her looks were elegant: long, straight, waist-length hair, Chinese features, proud and erect in stature, speech heavily accented with her Jamaican pronunciations of English.

In the early 1940s, my mother and father had a tumultuous relationship that evolved in fits and starts in Jamaica. It resumed when my African Jamaican father entered the United States illegally in 1945 to find my mother in Harlem. She thought she'd left him behind in Jamaica when she obtained a U.S. visa, but he stowed away on a merchant ship to New York City to persuade her to marry him. And so she did. She had escaped him and her painful memories of Jamaica by making her way to the United States in search of the American Dream and Gold Mountain, as the Chinese called America. She'd entered legally because, since her father was Chinese, she had received a visa after the Chinese Exclusion Acts were eased. China's alliance with the United States during World War II led to better immigration options for the Chinese to journey here.

Not surprisingly, their marriage dissolved seven years later when I was three years old, after my father had been discovered to be without legal documents and was deported to Jamaica. Two years later, he legally re-entered the United States because my mother became an American citizen. Her rights extended to her husband, so he could rejoin the family. But their distance and animosity were too great; their separation became permanent. She became a single mother and we became weekend visitors to our father's home in Springfield Gardens, Queens.

Similarly, my mother was separated from her father when she was three years old, living in Jamaica. But, unlike me, she never saw her father again.

"You don't know what it's like to grow up without the love of a father," is a sad refrain I recall my mother telling me throughout my life.

Why didn't she grow up with her father? Why didn't she grow up with her mother? Why don't we have relatives in Harlem like all the other kids? Where is my grandfather? Why are we Black and Chinese? Why did he leave? How can I help my Ma not be so sad?

These are the questions I asked not just as a young child, but throughout my life. I became a history and Black Studies major. I became an investigative journalist. I became a news director for NBC's largest TV station in the nation's largest TV market and my hometown, New York City. I moved on to become president of the NBC-owned station in Los Angeles, also overseeing their two Spanish-language stations because I was that good. I became the second African American female company officer in General Electric's 150-plus years. I became a wealthy investor and entrepreneur. I aimed my career and my financial plans at one goal: to find my mother's family in China, to seek the descendants of my grandfather Samuel Lowe, whose given name was Lowe Ding Chow.

Samuel Lowe later became a merchant, a shopkeeper in Jamaica. My mother knew this was his profession. I knew that she loved him, that she felt cheated out of a relationship with her father. I grew up feeling cheated out of a large family, out of cousins, aunts, uncles, grandmothers, and grandfathers. That was pretty much all I knew.

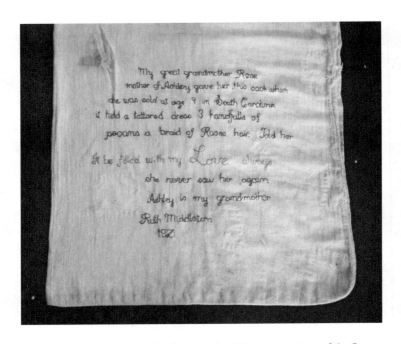

My great grandmother Rose
mother of Ashley gave her this sack when
she was sold at age 9 in South Carolina
it held a tattered dress 3 handfulls of
pecans a braid of Roses hair. Told her
It be filled with my Love always
she never saw her again
Ashley is my grandmother
Ruth Middleton
1921

What I now know is that I am in the 151st generation of the Lowe Clan of Lowe Swee Hap, Bao An, Guangdong Province, China. And I share a racial mixture with thousands, if not hundreds of thousands of people in the Americas—mixed race of the Asian and African diasporas, a people we colloquially call Blasian, for Black and Asian.

My Uncle Chow Woo named me Lowe Xiao Na. Lowe is my family's surname. Xiao means happiness and is the family's generation name that all females of my generation share. And my given name, Na, means beauty. Of all of the names that my dearest Uncle Chow Woo could have named his Black Hakka niece, he chose beauty, and I smile inside every time I think of it. We are so often taught that as Black women, we don't fit the standards of beauty that many in our society have adopted. And here, a Chinese patriarch meets his mixed-race, multicultural niece, and it is beauty he sees.

In 2012, I found my Hakka family. I found 300 of them—300

direct descendants of my grandfather, a man I never knew, whose picture I'd never seen, whose entire life story I'd never heard!

These family bonds transcend borders, race, and time. When I travel to Jamaica, to Ghana, and to China, I feel almost at home in those faraway lands as I do in Harlem. Even for those of us who were not born in China, we know we are born of China. We were not born in Africa, we know we are born of Africa. Slavery tried hard—yet unsuccessfully—to erase, to obliterate, to eradicate our families, our histories, our stories. My life tells one African American, African Jamaican, Hakka Chinese family's story that slavery wasn't able to silence.

Ever.

OUR INTERNAL WAR
EMBRACING A GREATNESS THAT SHOULD BE NORMAL
Aisha Hinds

Noted civil rights activist and feminist Audre Lorde wrote: "Sometimes we are blessed with being able to choose the time and the arena and the manner of our revolution, but more usually we must do battle wherever we are standing." That is true even when the battle is within ourselves, when we fight our naturalness to be great.

We live in a country built on the foundations of slavery. We are the fruits of centuries of seeds sown into the psyche of civilization. The human fabric of our nation is shaped and held in place by the perverse principles of enslavement. This perversion made the idea of a black or female president unusual and impossible when it should be normal, according to our Genesis genealogy, declaring we were all made in God's likeness and image. In spite of our convictions, a black president becomes a *THING*—a huge conquest of immeasurable significance.

My understanding of Genesis is that *ALL* of humanity was created in the IMAGO DEI (image of God), affording *ALL* a seat at the royal table awaiting an assignment garbed in greatness from our mighty, matchless Maker. One of the many fallouts from slavery is that it corrupts consciousness of this instinctual identity and has caused irrevocable damage through decades upon decades of divisive and destructive ideology. Creation commits a great sin to believe otherwise.

Women have historically been thought of as subservient, ancillary or softer spoken, and it's almost like the exception to a mythical rule that there are women who rise up and are seen as the agitators employing a different form of aggression in the fight against inequality and injustice. It is the likes of Mary McLeod Bethune, Rosa Parks, Sojourner Truth, Diane Nash, Angela Davis, Maya Angelou, and scores of other sisters who provide a paradigm for our present-day front-line femmes. The truth of the matter is whether you take a vocal approach or take an approach like that of a Harriet Tubman—strategically secretive using song to signal the next move—you are in the fight, "doing battle where you stand."

Harriet Tubman may not have been considered vocal or even visible, like Frederick Douglass. He was heavily photographed, while she moved in secret. She plotted her journey out of bondage sheltered by the darkness of night. Her plight revealed that not all battles are fought or won out in the open, and fortifies the idea that the black woman as a winning weapon isn't much of a secret but a proven fact.

The hard-fought battles that were exacerbated by the requirement to mobilize and strategize in secret or in the dark called for warriors who were indeed fearless and willing to die for the cause. Our greatest strengths as women have always lived in the ability to make insurmountable, selfless sacrifices for others, and most certainly for a cause greater than oneself. Women are caregivers by nature, willing to give the very last of self, tending to others. That one thing is notable about women throughout all of history. As such, "self-care" has become a novel necessity, inspiring scribes to devote volumes of their volition crafting manifestos about healing, harmony, balance, and sacred selfishness as survival tools for women. Instead of valuing faithful women warriors, a generational, genocidal curse rooted in the seeds of enslavement causes so many to disregard, disrespect, and dishonor the contributions of women of color to the fabric of this world. Subsequently, it creates a conversation in our minds littered with whispers of self-deprecating thoughts, which require us to continuously correct the narrative.

We have to work so hard to tell our stories, to fight for our truth, and convince listeners it is worth hearing and learning from. There is great value in revisiting our history, in all its forms, as a table of content and context for where the demise began and how we must draw from those who transcended. It saddens me to see those of us who have tapped out of any interest in revisiting our history, relinquishing a sacred part of self and collapsing in their consciousness as a casualty of the new narrative written for us. By new, that means anything after the origin of humanity that doesn't factor people of color as worthy, royal, and created in the exact likeness of the Creator, possessing power and purpose to exist in the world and be revered and respected. We've come so far. But it's almost as if the farther we come, the more we are continually reminded of how far we have to go.

The perversion of humanity as expressed in the edicts of enslavement has directly robbed an entire race of value, self-worth and a pure form of love, a right promised and owed since the genesis of creation.

I know.

I am a descendant of the many who were victims of grand theft identity. In my youth, I battled low self-esteem for many years. As an adult, I searched for answers and a cure for what I deemed to be as deadly as cancer. A lack of value for oneself inevitably paralyzes the ability to value another, and ultimate leads to a compromised existence on earth. My desire to perform in the fullness of what I was purposed and placed on this planet to do was crippled. I was afraid to be great, and I was also afraid to expect greatness from others. I learned to set my aim within a range of bare minimum to slightly above average. The idea of a Michelle Obama in the White House as First Lady to a Barack Obama was not even in the conversation. I hadn't yet realized or been "woke" enough to understand that I was the fruit of the seeds of slavery. I was systematically built to believe that black people are only allowed to be great once in a while, and that being great was not normal. Greatness was reserved for the exceptional. The words were always in my head: don't you dare try to be great, just settle for what you get. The disease of low self-worth manifested itself in the way I spoke to people, the way I treated people, how I behaved in school, the people from whom I chose to search for love, which was a direct reflection of how I treated myself—mediocre at best.

I was born in Brooklyn and raised among a huge Caribbean population—Jamaican, Haitian, Panamanian, Guyanese, Bajan, and Trinidadian. My immediate family came from Grenada. I didn't really know a world outside Brooklyn until I started to travel across the Brooklyn Bridge to LaGuardia High School in Manhattan. I felt that Brooklyn was an island, and all of these people were from that island. I didn't see color when I was growing up and didn't experience the distinction between black and white in an overt way. I went to school in an artistic environment, and it was one of those spaces that felt as if we were all unified and speaking a language that transcended race. Taking the train home with my white peers, I didn't even notice they were getting off at Seventh Avenue in Park Slope, and I kept going deeper into East Flatbush. It didn't register that we were living at two different social statuses because we were on the same train.

When I was sixteen, something tragic happened that would shift my life in a direction I never saw coming and thrust me to demand better of my life. One afternoon, on my way from school, wearing a hoodie that belonged to my boyfriend and a red coat on top of it, I was shot in my back a few feet from the entrance to my building. I heard the two shots that preceded the one that sent me face down to the ground, but I thought they were premature firecrackers in preparation for the Fourth of July, two months away. As I walked toward my building before being shot, I had two thoughts. The first was, Man, I'm tired; I don't want to go to Youth Meeting tonight (I had found community at a local church in East Flatbush called

Lenox Road Baptist Church, where I went to meet a boy and ended up becoming a member). The second was, I wonder who thinks it's July 4th.

In a split second, my Spirit nudged me to turn around, which is when I discovered that those weren't firecrackers; it was a group of young black men, one armed with a .45, chasing after a lone black boy who was running with his head ducked down. I turned to run, but hit the ground at the sound of the next gunshot. I attempted to get up and keep running, only to discover my body was unable to respond. That last shot had connected with me. I collapsed on the sidewalk waiting to die my inevitable death. According to the nightly news, I should have expected to die at sixteen. So I placed my forehead on my arm and waited for a news van rather than an ambulance. Spoiler alert: I didn't die. I lived, and I learned an invaluable truth about the presence and power of a pure love. I was laid up in Kings County Hospital for a week, and every person from every walk of my life came to visit. My white night-school teachers, my immigrant church leaders, my peers from the block, the neighboring blocks, across the bridge, other boroughs, the entire diaspora gathered at the foot of my hospital bed. I looked out at each one, bearing the pain of a grazed aorta and a removed right kidney, and saw LOVE. I knew it differently than I had ever known or read of it. I felt it, I smelled it, I tasted it, I was intoxicated by it. Their collective concern for my life affirmed that I mattered. There was a bigger picture, and I was supposed to get up from that bed and play my small part in a much larger narrative than the one I previously believed.

In the following months, I became deliberate in my pursuit of my purpose, to quell the fear of greatness, however it should articulate itself in my life. I survived the headlines, graduated from LaGuardia and went on to study theater at the University of Miami. Finding the courage to leave what was familiar to me—my family and my life in Brooklyn—I was driven by the remnant flickers of fire in the eyes of those people who willed me through my recovery after the shooting. I was convinced I had a right to discover the fullness of my truth as a black woman of faith on this earth, and do my best to leave it better than I found it somehow. I arrived at the campus of U.M. in a green-and-white checkered spaghetti-strap dress and some Timbs. (This outfit would define my approach to life for the rest of my days.) I learned about class distinction and minority vs. majority while in college. I entered the theater department, and I was one of only two black people in the entire department. All of the department faculty and professors were white, and there was no content that was reflective of my culture, of my story, of my experience, of my identity in the world. That was where I began to realize that we were on different planets. I didn't see myself in any of the material I was presented with to learn this craft. I knew better than to believe that narrative this time.

In our senior year, the university, for the first time in its history, put on an all-black production. It was George Wolfe's *The Colored Museum*, and there were just enough people enrolled at that time, from freshmen to seniors, to adequately cast an ensemble of black students to perform each role. It was revolutionary for the department and for the audiences coming to see our productions. Our university was known for its athletic department, and I took note of the number of football players and basketball players who willingly flocked to the theater on campus to see a play because there were people that looked like them on the stage. Shortly thereafter, I graduated with honors. I discovered my purpose in my passion for the arts and acting. I walked off that campus hoping I had, in some small way, left it better than when I came.

I think we're all on this planet playing a small part to a larger narrative. If we don't reach back and uproot those seeds of doubt planted in our beginnings, we will see ourselves only as weeds among flowers, manifestations of those seeds of unworthiness. That is a destructive kind of thinking that is contradistinctive to the truth of who we are.

There is such a rich history that defines us. When we accomplish a thing, we should realize that we were made, designed and destined to accomplish that thing. But because we live in a way that makes that part of the narrative an exception to the rule, we're always celebrating something that should actually be normal. Absolutely, Barack Obama should have been our president. That should be normal and expected. But we have lived so long in this oven of oppression that we're almost conditioned to believe that that is not our normal. It's abnormal. That's the matrix that we're living in. This is where we as people of color must begin to rise up and expectantly witness our strength, our intelligence, our innovative ideas and our spirit transcend.

I think of Harriet Tubman, who entered the world considered a piece of property, yet had woven into her an instinctual spirit for resistance and defiance. It wasn't necessarily taught to her. She just had a knowing that this ain't the way of things. Though she had no context for freedom, she was willing to put her life on the line, several times, in pursuit of it, and to facilitate that journey for others to experience what she believed was a birthright. She famously declared: "There was one of two things I had a right to, liberty or death; if I could not have one, I would have the other." We have an irrefutable right to be great, to live fearlessly in the fullness of our existence, to fight for freedom against systemic prejudices and perversions of policy. We begin where we are, with what we have and a willingness to do so selflessly.

What I have is my faith, my voice, and my art. As an artist, I aim to leave behind a canon of work that changes minds; that examines and exposes all levels of injustice; that explores our myriad articulations of sensuality, spirituality, and sexuality; that offers a voice for those who are sometimes overlooked, misunderstood, ostracized, or vilified; that is deliberate about inspiring youth; that pays homage and gratitude to our history, the ancestors, and my culture. I would that this body of work speak greatness into the generations that follow. May I take up my swords and heed the wisdom of Audre Lorde—DO BATTLE WHERE I AM STANDING and reach for the greatness in me that Genesis said is there.

THE FOOTPRINT OF AMERICA'S RACIAL STRUGGLE IN CUBA

DeWayne Wickham

In a 2009 open letter to Cuban President Raúl Castro, sixty prominent African Americans signed on to a stinging rebuke of the treatment of black civil rights activists in his country.

This letter and the response it produced are rooted in the muck of America's 246-year enslavement of people of African descent and the fight that is still being waged to secure racial equality for their descendants. While the cause is just, sometimes, the efforts to obtain it can go astray.

"We support Cuba's right to enjoy national sovereignty, and unhesitatingly repudiate any attempt at curtailing such a right," African American activists wrote to Castro. "However, at this historic juncture, we also do believe that we cannot sit idly by and allow for decent, peaceful and dedicated civil rights activists in Cuba, and the black population as a whole, to be treated with callous disregard for their rights as citizens and as the most marginalized people on the island.

"Racism in Cuba, and anywhere else in the world, is unacceptable and must be confronted," their missive concluded.

The most prominent signer of the letter was Dr. Cornel West, the acerbic public intellectual who once accused Barack Obama, the United States' first black president, of also being "the first niggerized black president" for not doing enough to fight "against white supremacy."

The open letter quickly drew a tart response from a group of prominent Cubans that included the noted Afro-Cuban poet-essayist Nancy Morejón and Esteban Morales, an acclaimed black economist and political scientist.

"A Yoruba proverb affirms, 'The lie may run for a year, but the truth will catch up with it one day,' " they wrote. "Although the most intolerant political circles and most powerful mass media have tried to impose a distorted image of contemporary Cuban society on the American public for a long time, in the end—in one way or another—reality will open the path."

In June 2010—during one of my twenty-five reporting trips to Cuba since 1999—I asked Morejón about this sparring. She softened her language without dulling her point.

"I don't want to look arrogant, especially with Cornel West. But I believe he sat on the side of something he doesn't actually know." West, she said, should have spoken to some of the leading blacks in Cuba before signing a letter that mischaracterized their struggle. "I believe that this dialogue that we haven't had is necessary," she said, wearily.

Shortly after I returned to the United States, I asked West if he was open to talking with Morejón about his letter and her response. He said he was. But now, nearly seven years later, that conversation still hasn't happened.

This missing dialogue is a collateral damage of American slavery and its continuing ripple effect throughout the American hemisphere. While blacks in the United States and Cuba have a common history of capture and enslavement, they traveled different paths to freedom.

In 1872—just seven years after the 13th Amendment to the Constitution ended slavery—Samuel R. Scottron, a black Brooklyn inventor, went to a Baltimore church to build support for Cuba's interracial fight against Spanish rule and its promise of freedom for Cuban slaves.

At the time, Cuba was home to more than five hundred thousand people of African descent. The Cuban rebel army was mostly black. Several of its senior commanders were black, including Antonio Maceo, a young "mulatto" general whose valor in combat earned him the nickname the Bronze Titan.

Scottron, the great-grandfather of famed singer, dancer and actress Lena Horne, was one of the founders of the Cuban Anti-Slavery Committee, which met on December 13, 1872, at Cooper Institute in New York City to rally support for Cuba's independence struggle.

Like those who penned the open letter to Castro, the group that took part in the Cooper Institute meeting included some of the leading black activists of the day. Among them, in addition to Scottron, were abolitionist Henry Highland Garnet; Howard Law School dean and future Virginia congressman John Mercer Langston; and James M. Trotter, the father of noted journalist William Monroe Trotter.

But the group's attempt to pressure the U.S. government to help Cuba floundered amid the fears of American businesses and southern racists that an independent Cuba with an interracial army might not be in their best interest—and the need for black activists in America to increasingly turn their attention to combating neo-slavery at home.

Slavery in Cuba was abolished in 1886. But, as in the United States, the undertow of slavery has persisted.

A riptide of racial bigotry and political deal-making in the United States ended Reconstruction and gave birth to the Ku Klux Klan and a century of Jim Crow laws and practices, which have been followed by the current Jim Crow Jr. era—a kinder, gentler form of racism that masks the long reach of slavery's shadow.

This ripple effect of American slavery has impacted relations between Cubans of African descent and African Americans in at least two important ways.

One: It caused many black activists in the United States to lose touch with the events that spawned the creation of an all-black political movement in Cuba shortly after it gained independence from Spain and an American occupying force.

Two: It moved some black activists, like those who signed the 2009 letter to Raúl Castro, to view the struggle for racial equality in Cuba through the myopic lens of their own fight to achieve that victory in the United States.

In my travels across Cuba—trips on which I've met hundreds of Cubans in their homes, offices, and playgrounds and on the streets of cities from Santiago de Cuba to Havana—the vast majority of people of African descent I've encountered support the Castro government.

Many of them know the history of the brutal suppression of black veterans of the Cuban War of Independence (which Americans call the Spanish-American War) at the beginning of the 20th century. They know that thousands of these black men were massacred in the spring of 1912 near the eastern tip of Cuba by government forces backed by U.S. warships and troops. Though the Americans didn't take part in the slaughter, they prevented these black veterans from fleeing Cuba to nearby Haiti.

For the next 47 years, a succession of white-dominated governments ruled Cuba. They perpetuated the racial exclusion and segregationist practices that the black veterans had protested. During the guerrilla campaign that brought him to power in 1959, Fidel Castro promised Cubans of African descent a better life—something he largely delivered on when he came to power.

The U.S. civil rights movement is a campaign against slavery's rear guard, people who disguise their true purpose in talk of states' rights and small government. But in Cuba the fight for civil rights is compounded by the fact that, for nearly sixty years, the United States has tried to topple the government.

Dissidents inside Cuba—both black and white—are widely supported by forces in the United States, the country that continues to try to strangle the economic life out of Cuba.

"None of the governments prior to 1959 did anything for the

poor in general or for blacks in particular," Esteban Morales wrote in a 2013 HavanaTimes.org posting. "Instead, the previous authorities ruled the country for the benefit of a few, with all the machinery and tools of a neocolonial administration that maintained racism and racial discrimination, corruption and poverty, displaying the model of exploitation and control that the U.S. had designed for the island."

Morales is no communist sycophant. He can be trusted to speak truth to power.

In 2010, he was kicked out of Cuba's Communist Party for publicly saying that "corruption" was much more dangerous to the country's existence than "the so-called internal dissidents." He was reinstated a year later without apologizing for those words.

Like the signers of the open letter to Raúl Castro, Morales is committed to eradicating all remaining vestiges of slavery. But he sees this struggle as one that, though fueled by American hegemony, requires a uniquely Cuban solution.

That thought, no doubt, will dominate the discussion Nancy Morejón hopes to have one day with Cornel West.

LEMONADE
THE DUALITY OF A BLACK WOMAN'S DEVOTION IN THE SHADOW OF SLAVE CULTURE

Tonya M. Matthews

The opening scene spans images of new grass and old stones.
The camera pans the stone tunnel leading to a doorway. It
was once a captured fort used as a Union Army training
ground for freed slaves, but the sight reminds me of my trip
to castle forts that held captured peoples being sent across
to become slaves. Various renditions of "Are you cheating on
me?" punctuate shots of plantation imagery from beginning to
end, from indictment to forgiveness. Seriously? Are we really
throwing it all the way back to slavery to find the strength
and reason to survive another episode of wanton infidelity
and emotional abuse in the story of our ever-elusive heroine:
Black Love? What's with all the comingling of husbands, uncles, daddies, and mothers' fathers? Did the Queen B just slip
in a shout-out to blood memory? If that's the case, I'm loving

all the water imagery, but clearly I'm going to need a drink
much stronger than that.
— *Scenes from* Lemonade *shot at Fort Macomb, a 19th-century
brick fort in Louisiana*

Dearly Beloved, we have gathered here today to figure out why I
can't get past the first three minutes of Beyoncé's *Lemonade* video
album without coming to tears, and why I can't make it more than
four or five lines into any of Warsan Shire's poems running through
that docudrama without a half-cussing, teeth-sucking, hallelujah-
chorusin' fit. As I am not part of the Beyhive, my halo of bubbled-up
emotion is not about an overabundance of empathy for a woman I
don't actually know or even follow on Twitter. Or is it?

Let me warn you: This is not about to be an anthropological social
sciences thesis on the multi-generational impact of enslavement on
the disintegration of family constructs within a culture or the persistent institutionalization of the mentality that made this possible
and inevitable.

Rather this is just me—a fairly accomplished, relatively sane,
mostly kind, and generally joyful Black woman—about to ask herself
some pretty dangerous questions. I have seen sisters bruised through
to the soul and broken down to the spirit-ankles on a Saturday night
get back up on Monday morning and sprint twenty miles because
there is work to be done. And she's still probably planning to cook
dinner and keep it sexy for the brother responsible for all them soul-
shattering shenanigans when he comes home. I have been in this
space myself and can only admit this without complete humiliation
because I am not alone.

I'm not talking about physical abuse. (That is an entirely different
conversation, for which no disparate bassline and haunting plantation baptism scene can ever inspire sympathy for the perpetrator.)
This is about the kind of abuse that comes from the constant mental gymnastics and heartache salving required to maintain the idea

that "just coming home" is the gold standard for African American relationships.

On top of all that, we seem to live in a space assuming some kind of infinite, ancestral source to a Black woman's resilience and patience. I was once just the strongest, the most loyal, and the ultimate ride-or-die; now I'm also, apparently, magical. There is a thin line between confidence and pressure.

Second warning: I've got more questions than I do answers.

The echoes of slave norms and survival instincts are often cited as the fuel of pervasive bad behavior of African American men when it comes to home and family in our community. But if the Black man's actions are tied to those roots, aren't the responses of Black women tied to those same roots?

My husband and I are both products of the bones—the ones resting at the bottom of the Atlantic, the ones fertilizing the trees from which they were hung, and the ones dancing under gravestones because Yes, We Did! get ourselves a Black president with a Black wife. But he and I reflect those bones very differently—most times in opposition to each other. Once in a while, I feel we are having an argument that is not ours alone.

I shared the premise of this new, personal, and confounding inner monologue with Dr. Johnnetta Cole, the accomplished anthropologist and thought leader. I jokingly asked her if she could answer my questions in the two minutes we had before stepping into a meeting. Her response was unexpected, profound, and challenging. She said: "I applaud you for looking into this from a personal perspective. There are whole volumes of academic uncovering, but we cannot understand and heal that which we do not interrogate for ourselves. Just because you have lived it doesn't mean you have interrogated it. Keep on this path."

Damn. Damn. Damn.

"When life gives you lemons, make lemonade" is a proverbial phrase used to encourage optimism and a positive can-do attitude in the face of adversity or misfortune. Lemons suggest sourness or difficulty in life, while lemonade is a sweet drink." Wikipedia and a grandmother's kitchen table.

Admittedly, I'm trying to excavate a mountain with a spoon. So let me start with one small mouthful, a small bite, as in one horrifyingly powerful construct of slavery at a time. Here goes:

What happens when you can't depend upon your man to come home because there are a hundred legitimate reasons he could not come home? He could be traded—sold to pay a debt, sold for a good price or lost in a bet. He could be dead—whipped to death, worked to death, or hanged because the wrong relative of the master got drunk that day. He could be kept out of the home because the master had decided to breed you. He could be taken out of the home because the master simply said so, and your man was powerless to do anything about it. Or maybe he didn't come because it was the day and, according to plan, he ran and, hopefully, he'd make enough on the other side to send for you.

That's a whole lot of lemons. You got to bring a special kind of sugar—and a lot of it—to make a fruit that strange potable. I would say that, in an environment like that, simply coming home becomes its own kind of miracle. I would say that an environment like that creates a space within women so sickeningly sweet that we can use the bitterness of that instability to transform this most basic thing of coming home into something holy.

However, when those hundred different legitimate reasons disappear, and when the ability to honor home is within the realm of personal control, the act of coming home reverts from subtly miraculous to appropriately basic. What, then, will it take for us to stop worshiping the act?

Before I step into this space, let me acknowledge that I am a believer. I believe in Black Men, Black Love, Black Staying Power, and Black Girl Magic. I was raised to do so, and I have plenty of examples to back up my belief. That said, I am perplexed by the elusiveness of the first three believables and the necessity of the last.

Around my late twenties, early thirties, I began to define a "good man" as one with fewer children by fewer women and, when applicable, with an appropriate paperwork-type divorce rather than a "just walk away from it all" type of divorce. In retrospect, I was setting a (low) standard for how many homes he could abandon before coming to mine. In my thirties, I began to understand that "good home training" had to be evaluated not only by how a man treats his mother but also by how badly he had treated his ex and how long she had let him get away with it. In other words, I began to look for evidence that he had been held accountable for coming home.

It's all just "a laugh a tear" these days. We all know the stories. Be it from your brokenhearted girlfriend; the embittered, recently divorced college roommate; the friend of your wife/sister/cousin who talks way too much; or during your morning commute as Steve Harvey rants poetic over another sad, sad Strawberry Letter. These are stories of women worshiping the potential comeback, like some tired sports hero movie.

There's the one about the man who married one woman while engaged to another. Still, the jilted fiancée is worried about hurting him so doesn't mention the child. She knows he's wrong, but he sounds so sincere in the texts he still sends her.

Then there's the sister who stalled her career—though she still paid the mortgage—while raising their two kids so he could finish his degree. A good degree in his portfolio and a few extra pounds on her hips later, he complains that "something's changed" and files for divorce. She calls this a midlife crisis and waits.

And let me not throw shade, as if I have none. Let me throw my story in the game: dated a man for three years, drawers for his stuff in my house and all. When we started that relationship, he had three kids—when it ended, he had five. None of those children are mine, and he did not have twins.

I have heard it said that the legacy of enslaved African men being raised and rented out as studs, with the enslaved African women's "beauty" being recognized only when sexually desirable to the master, is related to the African American community's celebrated mythology of the pimp. Is pimpdom the generational translation of being singularly valued for your ability to impregnate women, be impregnated, and be sexual without the requirement of "home"? Is having multiple "babies' mommas" the haunting consequence of being rented out from plantation to plantation and placed in temporary, contractual, commodity-based contexts with woman after woman? Is this the ghost of keeping arms-length from the definition of home because it was unreliably defined, never truly yours, and therefore home is wherever you decide to show up? This line of reasoning lays the burden of the instability of Black Love at the feet of Black men.

Maybe. But what is the consequence of being generationally trained to value the simple act of your man coming home above all else? It could not be about when he came home; it could not be about how he came home. It could never be about what was done when he was out of the home. Speaking evil of the deeds done that allowed him to come home alive in the first place was always . . . pointless. Who does a woman have to become to allow just coming home to be enough? What part of this transformation contributes to the instability of Black relationships in the generations that come after the original reason why? If Black women continue to prioritize the act of simply coming home—without requirements for accountability, fidelity, support, claiming and naming of home—are we just as, if not more, accountable for the elusiveness of true home that we rail against?

> *No problem can be solved from the same level of consciousness that created it.*
> — Albert Einstein, genius

> *A freed slave with a shackled mind is a dangerous thing.*
> — JaHipster, poet

Clearly there was a time when Black women had to stay as a matter of survival. His. Hers. Ours. And that was a time when we understood the staying and did not question it.

But are we still in such a time?

Maybe. God bless America; the land that I love . . . is still making it hard for a Black man to come home. The brothers are still being used for target practice. We've moved from halfhearted prosecution and investigation to turning cops "unjustifiable homicides" into cause celebs when they've killed the Black men they are sworn to protect. Black mothers must still raise their sons in ways that minimize the lynchings. There are still too many days when our men don't come home because of circumstances beyond their control. There are many more days when the men themselves worry they may not come home, struggle to define home, face one more barrier created to keep them from home.

Therefore, this is still such a time. So, if the sisters' role is to simply stand still and be the new North Star guiding the brothers home, let's do it.

But is that healthy for Black women?

Maybe not. OK, probably not. Is it worthwhile for us to stay if we lose faith while doing it? We have created a righteous schizophrenia that is surely the source of migraines and high blood pressure. Every man should be left if he doesn't treat a sister right—except for your man. He just needs more time. I can tell my girlfriend to file those papers and get out, but I can no longer pretend I don't understand why she stays. In both cases, we are too quick to become comfortable with the instinct to save relationships and too slow to question them. We must now question our lackluster definition of home in the context of these resonant, but still different times. We take this all too far if our resilience becomes a substitute for forgiveness and our patience a stand-in for accountability.

Not being able to require a man to define home for himself and to have faith that he will is dangerously debilitating for a woman. Moreover, we pass on that faithlessness as easily as family recipes, creating a standard of no-standard for both our daughters and sons to live up to. So, don't do it.

Anyone got a tiebreaker?

This is as close as I can get: I've seen Black women in action. Our tenacity and strength is ridiculous—also a legacy. Let's not forget that we, too, were in the fields. Through all of this—then and now—Black women have been the sustaining source of stability, even as the peculiar institution attempted to strip it from our community. We are home. So we must continue to be home. Yes, we are the modern North Star.

So, I acknowledge that our devotion is necessary, but I do not believe it is sufficient.

A pattern of reward without responsibility makes Black women as culpable in perpetuating the elusiveness of Black Love as anyone else. Blood memory or not, we need to balance out all this resiliently patient home-making with something ... before we are fully exhausted.

After all, our community is here. We had a president. We have a few C.E.O.s. And we even got a monument and a museum on the Mall in D.C. African Americans have been dealt some serious lemons, and we surely whipped up an incredible lemonade, a drink worthy of our optimism and capable of our healing.

But, from my perspective at this moment, Black women are the source of the sweetness. How much longer can we be?

IT'S NOT JUST HAIR
T'Keyah Crystal Keymáh

In 1990, on the sketch variety show *In Living Color*, I wore natural hairstyles at the end of every episode, when the cast came out as "ourselves." Since no one in the television industry seemed to have any experience creating styles from the motherland, I rocked the *self*-styled twists that slowly ushered into fashion a new wave of modern-day naturalistas.

In the time since, I have had countless conversations about hair: my hair, other people's hair, the history of Black women's hair, and so on. In an effort to answer many questions at once, while changing the tone of those conversations, I included the meat of some of those talks in my book on natural hairstyles, "Natural Woman/Natural Hair." Acknowledging my status as a natural hair icon, a journalist wondering what all of the fuss was about once commented, "It's just hair!"

The thing is, it is not.

It's not just hair. I stood nearly alone in 1990, amid a growing obsession with weaves. The conversions to my side of the beauty parlor were slow going, even in that short-lived period of pseudo-cultural freedom, because we were not just "Four Hundred Years Without a

Comb," we were four hundred years without a compliment. So complete was our multigenerational brainwashing that many women, even today, see no connection between the historic representations of textured hair as ugly, dirty, difficult, or otherwise negative, and their own aversion to it.

Like it or not, our hair is a 3-D animated billboard that advertises the degree to which we display our acceptance or rejection of the genetically instilled and ubiquitously corroborated lesson that our success, if not our survival, is dependent upon our physical acceptability and/or inconspicuousness. In general, a person's hair says, "I am clean or dirty, organized or messy, fashionable or unaware, free-spirited or conservative, rich or poor."

For Black women, however, our hair also says, "I am safe or a threat to White people; a source of pride or embarrassment to Black people; a perpetuator of a Eurocentric or an Afrocentric standard of beauty."

Even some women who consider themselves natural cannot bring themselves to actually be so. So many have come to me bragging about having given up relaxers, then sharing that they press or blow dry their hair, simply because it is easier to comb that way. Well, of course it is, if you are using a comb designed for straight hair! They tell me that the weave is for protection, while their natural hair grows out. Of course it is for protection. They are protecting themselves from the backlash of having short, natural hair!

Beyond the cultural implications are the physical and economic ones. Black women spend billions of dollars a year on hair products that cause great damage to our hair and scalps. Since skin is porous, it is a short leap to assume that the harsh chemicals used to tame the texture of our hair are also contributing to our higher rates of cancer and brain-born physical anomalies. As women of African descent, our hair, historically, is the opposite of that of our oppressors. Why then, would we seek hair care from people with hair that is the opposite of our own, and who have demonstrated a disdain for us and our well-being? Is it because we have not yet broken that habit of counting on our oppressors for sustenance and affirmation, however unfulfilling, that was developed during the enslavement of our ancestors? Finally, there's the attitude of hair being about fun, fashion, and freedom of choice. I'm all for that. When we, as a people, however, consistently and defiant of fad and era, define fun, fashion, and/or freedom as the conversion of our crowns to mimic that of our oppressors, historic and present, then something is wrong. When we further ignore that this habit makes billionaires of those outside of our community, while sometimes causing us irreparable harm, something is wrong, and it's not our hair.

It is not just hair.

It's a tool of cultural, economic, and sometimes physical suicide.

THE WEAPON OF NARRATIVE AND THE AFRICAN AMERICAN STORY

Michael Simanga

A few years ago I was in Bentonville, Ark., to give a talk sponsored by Black Art in America on African American creativity and artistic production. While I was there, I walked through a beautiful green space to find the Crystal Bridges Museum of American Art. Funded by the Walton Family Foundation (Walmart), it is a significant addition to modern museums, both architecturally and artistically. I wandered around for most of the afternoon, soaking in the expansive collection and observing the responses of other people to the art. There were hundreds of people, but I saw only a handful of African Americans or other people of color that afternoon. As I was walking out, a young white couple asked me what I thought. I smiled at them and said, "It is a testament to how important art and museums are, but in the Crystal Bridges Museum of American Art, where are the rest of the Americans?"

They didn't immediately understand what I was saying. In that museum of American art, the artists chosen by the founders and curators as representative of America were almost exclusively white and male. Absent were African Americans, Native Americans, Hispanic Americans, Asian Americans—and I don't remember seeing the work of any women of color. After some quick reflection, the young couple responded positively and acknowledged that it hadn't occurred to them. They walked away with a look that indicated they were either in deep contemplation about the issue or I'd just ruined their day by bringing up a myth-shattering truth: This is not a white country. Never has been. Never will be.

The true greatness of America is the evidence of the peoples of the world, representations of the human family flowing from Africa evolving to the awe-inspiring array of color from all over the globe. Diverse faiths and languages, the stories from the indigenous and those carried on the decks or in the bottoms of ships crossing the oceans, are all in the America of all the Americans.

Historical narrative and how it is projected into the world is a question of power. Power decides who wields the authority to create, authenticate and tell their version of events. For African Americans, the traditional narrative of our country is an example of two dialectical forces bound in the ebb and flow of a war over the territory of story that begins with the kidnapping and enslavement of the first Africans brought to these shores and continues in the 21st century.

The 246-year enslavement of Africans and their descendants in the colonies and the United States required not just the physical destruction and exploitation of a large part of Africa but the destruction of the memory of Africa and its people for those enslaved. Traders and brutal owners wiped away the idea of people being equal members of the human family and great contributors to world civilization. It had to be replaced with the mythology of Africa as an uncivilized continent of ignorant heathens running around naked, engaged in cannibalism, and without knowledge of the true God. Slavery was one of the most horrific and devastating atrocities in human history, and a narrative had to be created to justify and reconcile it to the religious beliefs of the perpetrators, those complicit and those benefitting from crimes that Frederick Douglass once said "would disgrace a nation of savages."

To further solidify a rationale for the crime of slavery, white superiority and black inferiority were cast as divine will and the natural order. In his Cornerstone Speech—one of the defining documents in the founding of the Confederacy—Alexander Stephens, vice president of the Confederacy through the Civil War, reiterated: "With us, all of the white race, however high or low, rich or poor, are equal in the eye of the law. Not so with the negro. Subordination is his place. He, by nature, or by the curse against Canaan, is fitted for that condition which he occupies in our system."

The refining and retelling of the lies evolved into a complex system of ideas that reproduced and contributed cultural artifacts such as the Confederate flag that projects the false notion of white supremacy.

What becomes history is usually a factual and fictive tale told and repeated by those with the power to transfer the narrative to the world through all of the institutions they control. It is like rap music sold at Walmart—the clean version with the rhythm, but devoid of the rhyme that houses the pain, the rage, the demand to be heard from deep down near the bottom. The historical narrative of white supremacy minimizes the extreme violence done to the exploited black lives whose labor produced wealth and progress while denying them the benefits. The sanitized and mythologized version of slavery and its perpetual scars permeates all American institutions and culture. It became and often remains woven into the practices of faith institutions and the rituals of government. It lives in the media we know and finds expression in new media as it evolves. Across the span of generations it is a tale told as truth that has to be disturbed and disrupted.

There has always been Black resistance to the white supremacist narrative. It came from those whose experience in the same historical geography did not conform to the story being told by those whose power was wielded against them. As an example, the first wave of black literary response in the United States to enslavement was a body of work known as the slave narratives. Those firsthand accounts of the real yet unimaginable dehumanization of black people in enslavement as told by Frederick Douglass, Anna Julia Cooper, Harriet Ann Jacobs, Booker T. Washington, and others was a stunning contrast and rebuke to the accepted view of the benevolence of slavery. Their voices stood in sharp contrast to those who engaged or benefited from the exploitation and oppression of Africans and their descendants.

The fight of black people to be recognized and treated as human beings, equal members of the human family, as co-citizens in the country of their birth and choice is manifested not only in the physical confrontation with institutions of power through protest, insurrection and social movements but also in the unyielding assertion of their own voice and from their own experience. From the slave narratives to the chant "Black Lives Matter," the African American voice has forced itself into the national conversation refusing generation after generation, only to be silenced. In that spirit, Richard Allen founded the African Methodist Episcopal Church. From that assertion, the brilliant Black historian Carter G. Woodson created Negro History Week, which eventually developed into Black History Month. Out of that tradition came the National Council of Negro Women and Black sororities and civic clubs. The Harlem Renaissance and the Black Arts Movement gave form and movement to cultural resistance and creative platforms. In the poetry of Gwendolyn Brooks, the essays of James Baldwin, and the novels of Toni Morrison, and in the music of John Coltrane, Nina Simone, and Motown, it is the authentic voice of African Americans, the progeny of enslaved Africans and their descendants who refused to remain the unheard. In the cadences of the sermons of Dr. Martin Luther King and the influences of jazz in the speeches of Malcolm X, the undeniable voice of Africa reaches out, forces its way into the consciousness of African Americans and the world.

In their own chronicle, in their own voice, Black people are not creatures created by a divinity to be brutalized and enslaved for generations to produce wealth for others. Their telling was of black strength of body and spirit, mind and imagination, to survive the atrocity of slavery with its instruments of control, torture, sexual assault, and other forms of legal and extralegal violence. In their songs and poems, their dances and worship rituals, they passed on the conviction that it was a victory to stay alive. The God of their beliefs gave them the sacred mantra passed from generation to generation: "If not me, my children. If not my children, their children. If not those children, their children, but one day we will be free."

Generation after generation must hold on to distant knowledge that enslavement was not always their condition. Generation after generation must pass on the faith that they and others would end it one day. Their story is also of searching, of needing a beginning, an ontology and epistemology that connects them to a sacred under-standing based on justice and knowledge that precedes the period of enslavement. African Americans needed—and still need—to end the wandering in humiliation that comes from being disconnected from a point of origin that precedes the time before Africa's great disaster of the slave trade and colonialism. It is a search for a truer self as a way to confront being forced to wear the cloak of an inferior self. For the American descendants of enslaved Africans, the restoration of the collective self begins in Africa.

John Henrik Clarke, the Pan-Africanist writer, historian, and pioneer in the creation of Africana studies, wrote: "History, I have often said, is a clock that people use to tell their political time of day. It is also a compass that people use to find themselves on the map of human geography. History tells a people where they have been and what they have been. It also tells a people where they are and what they are. Most importantly, history tells a people where they still must go and what they still must be. There is no way to go directly to the history of African Americans without taking a broader view of Af-rican world history."

In human history, the atrocities we commit against our sisters and brothers are always justified but not justifiable. We create stories to provide moral and theological, legal, political and economic, and even pseudoscientific validation for the horrific acts we sling upon one another. An atrocity on the scale of slavery in the United States required a narrative that had to begin with the denigration of Africa. The necessary lie that Africa, Africans, and their descendants are inherently inferior continues to be problematic in American life and culture. But it is the institutional imposition of inferiority that has cast black people as a persistent peripheral population, pushed to the margins and positioned there as proof that they don't belong in the center. And that condition persists in large part because the true story of Africans and their descendants remains untold, distorted or barely mentioned in the way we teach our children. In world history, our children are focused on the accomplishment of Europe with minor mention of Asia and Africa, with the exception of Egypt. In U.S. history there is minimal attention to the foundational and intricate ways that the labor and gifts of black people contributed mightily to America's status as the most powerful country in the history of the world.

Even in the 21st century, too often our story rests on the mythological United States, not on its great truth. This country has moved forward when it pushes toward the ideas expressed in its founding documents. When we reach into the deep folds of the history, even the periods of shame like slavery and genocide against native peoples, and understand the heroism of the men and women who fought for the society of equality and justice, progress comes. When it retreats to the false narrative, when it compromises with those ideas, when it deprives some of its people their humanity or their citizenship, our old habits rise up from the lies to snatch the narrative back out of the throats of those whose demand is for the truth.

In a statement to white Americans, Albert Einstein said: "Your ancestors dragged these black people from their homes by force; and in the white man's quest for wealth and an easy life they have been ruthlessly suppressed and exploited, degraded into slavery. The modern prejudice against Negroes is the result of the desire to maintain this unworthy condition. . . . I believe that whoever tries to think things through honestly will soon recognize how unworthy and even fatal is the traditional bias against Negroes."

Einstein begins with the recognition of a home, an existence of black people in Africa before the slave trade. He includes reference to the violence of slavery, its intent and enduring influence. He ends with a comment that continues to ring true today. The truth has to be recognized and embraced. Failure to do so is fatal.

The term African American began to gain widespread use during Jesse Jackson's historic campaign for president in 1988. It has become the officially acceptable and standard descriptor for descendants of the Africans who were enslaved in the United States. It is not just a convenient title on a demographic survey. Rather, it is a reminder— a daily reminder—of the important bond between Africa and America through the descendants whose experience includes both. It is an endorsement of the important assertion of the right of African Americans to be respected as human beings whose deep and ancient history is as much a critical part of their identity as is their experience in America. To justify the system of slavery, a white supremacist mythology, historiography, theology, pedagogy, and culture was created. The suppression of Africa's history and contributions to the world is an enduring barrier to the expression of the full human and civil rights of African Americans and the emergence of a fully inclusive diverse democratic country. It is our duty as citizens to ensure not just that Africa is said daily when we refer to African Americans, but that the truth of its value is brought in to the narrative of the United States as an equally important contributor to the making of this nation.

As Ida B. Wells said, "The way to right wrongs is to turn the light of truth upon them."

OUR NEW CIVIL RIGHTS MOVEMENT WILL BEGIN IN OUR SCHOOLS

Torrance G. Latham

Slavery is insidious and as deeply woven into the fabric of American culture as the red, white and blue on its symbolic flag.

How do I know? I'm only twenty-five, but I am enslaved.

I am bound by the knowledge that I live with the legacy of a system that has worked to diminished me.

In my short life, I have learned about the mass incarceration of black men.

In my short life, I have learned about the ballistic lynching of black bodies by some law enforcement officers.

These are the lessons I learned in a public school system that barely taught me half of what I needed to know to survive. I taught myself the rest.

What I have learned most is that America wants me to learn about my history least of all.

Yes, America has found unconscionable comfort in historical amnesia to racism. That has led to the nurturing of enablers of white supremacy who question the impact that race plays in the 21st century. Or do not care what role it plays.

Mentally, racism is toxic. Morally, it is uncouth.

And the idea that we refuse to accept that it was birthed in slavery, that it is undeniably a continuation of slavery, that it keeps some people living in slavery, is exasperating.

Look at how we are educated:

I have watched policy decisions from our imperialist nation that have led to the decimation of public schools, where mostly black and brown bodies learn. Minorities represent more than 50 percent of the public school population, according to the National Center for Education Statistics. Yet less than 20 percent of the teachers come from communities of color. White teachers are thrown into minority-dominated communities, where some have no interests besides collecting a paycheck. They are, in many cases, forced to teach black children a whitewashed history with the most appalling, limited resources available.

Because the truth about American history does not make for palatable optics politically, black and white children are robbed of learning uncomfortable truths about slavery and its residual impact when their minds are most fertile. America's educational system has insufficiently taught its students about the exploitation and unabashed hatred white supremacists have had for those with whom they do not identify. Meanwhile, the American government functions seamlessly as the predatory system designed to keep the public ill-informed, pro–Western civilization, and under control.

Black communities must look outside traditional means of education. We must collectively dig deeper into our history. Black communities also need more educators dedicated to challenging false historical ideologies. Black youth will not fully understand where they're going without knowing the sacrifices their ancestors made for our freedom and how resilient we are as people.

The values of critical thinking and reading comprehension must be reasserted in our culture. Instead, we are constantly asked to sit down and discuss race with people who represent the values of white supremacy. Humanity should not be debated. The purpose of those conversations is to discredit your real-life experiences and narratives. There is no intention of true fairness and justice.

It is no coincidence that Donald Trump, a reality-show star, is now president. He ran a propaganda-driven campaign fueled by bigotry, homophobia, xenophobia, and misogyny. He is the byproduct of a celebrity-driven, anti-intellectual culture currently at its peak. Entertainment over substance has become a malignant tumor in the development of our society. It provides many with an escape from the social ills surrounding us daily. From the food we consume to the religion our faiths have been based upon, a subconscious commitment to white validation has left an indelible imprint on black culture.

Until all American students are taught from an early age the complexities of American history, empathy will lag far behind in a capitalistic society predicated on self-interests. The indifference, hate, and exploitation of black lives date back to antebellum slavery. But the outcome of indifference, hate, and exploitation for black bodies is the loss of life by way of death or prison cell.

The new slavery is rampant poverty that a Republican-driven Congress wants to perpetuate. Impoverished families in predominantly black and brown inner cities watch their children suffer while privileged families send their children to private and/or suburban schools. Black people from all classes are tired of seeing innocent men, women, and children murdered by the police, whose salary is paid by those they prey upon.

The fate of black children has been tied to people who view them as less than human. We must change our own narratives. America's domestic priorities and national character are in need of a rapid transformation. Empathy must be equal for all, not just when it serves one's self-interest. A focus on federal government policies is important, but we must not neglect the state legislatures whose decisions directly impact our lives. Local electorates' feet need to be held to the fire. If opportunistic politicians are unable to provide receipts for their rhetoric, remove them when it's time to cast another ballot. Our kids and communities are relying on us to be civically and socially engaged.

If we are to value our futures, we must embrace self-awareness. We must fight for the dignity and confidence that should come from the memory of how resilient black people are and have been in America.

We, as young black Americans, must question everything, think critically, organize our ideas, mobilize with like-minded individuals, and, while resisting, focus on building our communities from the grass roots.

Every black student attending an American public school that is teaching them nothing about our history must teach himself or herself to ensure a free future.

There is no need to fantasize about what you would've done had you lived in the civil rights' golden era.

This is the new civil rights era.

We are the movement.

History is watching, and our defining moment is now.

THE BLACK PRESS—
MORE NEEDED THAN EVER

Herb Boyd

The Black press and slavery are inextricably linked in our nation's tumultuous history. Past is prologue, and the press is one of the ways we "got ovah" slavery.

When John Russwurm and Samuel Cornish conceived and published *Freedom's Journal*, the first African American newspaper in America, in 1827, the masthead declared its mission unequivocally: "We wish to plead our own cause. Too long have others spoken for us. Too long has the public been deceived by misrepresentations, in things which concern us dearly."

Nothing concerned the editors more dearly than slavery on that spring day of March 16, 1827, when the first issue of the paper was published. While the editors promised to address a myriad of injustices, they let their readers know that "we would not be unmindful of our brethren who are still in the iron fetters of bondage."

Four months after *Freedom's Journal* was launched, enslaved adult men and women were emancipated in New York, where the *Journal* was founded. If the celebration was muted, it may have been because of the proviso that the children of the enslaved were bound to serve a twenty-five- to-twenty-seven-year indentured term to their former masters. This condition did not go without outrage from the paper.

Nor was it unsparing of the Black bondage beyond New York. During its two years of existence, the paper was relentless in its opposition to slavery, lynching, and other civil and human rights restrictions imposed on African American citizens. *Freedom's Journal* would spur the rise of a number of Black newspapers, broadsides, and articles by abolitionists, few more fervent and passionate than David Walker. His *Appeal*, published a year after the demise of the *Journal*—a paper that ran one of his most famous declarations—was in several ways a conduit to the succeeding publications, though Walker would side with Cornish after he and Russwurm differed over the role of the colonization movement.

"I adopt the language of the Rev. S. E. Cornish," Walker espoused, supporting the minister's publication *The Rights of All*. "Any coloured man of common intelligence, who gives his countenance and influence to that colony, further than its missionary object and interest extend, should be considered as a traitor to his brethren, and discarded by every respectable man of colour."

The split between Cornish and Russwurm, while they both remained unwavering antislavery advocates, anticipated the parting of company between Frederick Douglass and Martin Delany. Their relationship began in 1848, when Delany joined Douglass's *North Star* as a co-editor after the failure of his own abolitionist paper, the *Mystery*. This formidable duo worked together for only a year or so, until Delany resigned. A philosophical divergence between Delany and Douglass had become untenable. Moreover, Douglass was against the colonization movement—the idea that the best future for Black Americans was to emigrate—a position Delany favored.

For the most part, this was Delany's last venture into journalism, though he became a fairly productive author of books. Meanwhile, Douglass continued to publish antislavery newspapers, including *Frederick Douglass's Paper* (1851–60), *Douglass' Monthly* (1860–63), and the *New National Era* (1870–74). Of these, none were more important than *Frederick Douglass's Paper*, since it began shortly after the Fugitive Slave Act of 1850 was passed, making the lives of Blacks, in bondage or not, all the more harrowing and perilous.

Drawing on his inspiration from William Lloyd Garrison, the publisher of the *Liberator* and a believer in the tactic of moral suasion, Douglass kept to his motto of abolishing slavery and improving the condition of "free colored people in the North." It was a unique abolitionist paper that often featured proslavery stories, if only to counter them with one in opposition to the story. Douglass was by no means of that ilk of radical abolitionists, best represented by John Brown, but he never cowered in speaking out against what many called the "peculiar institution."

A famed statesman and author of three autobiographies, Douglass didn't shrink from assailing other significant institutions. "In respect to the Church and the government, we especially wish to make ourselves fully and clearly understood," he wrote in the pages of his paper. "With the religion of the one, and the politics of the other, our soul shall have no communion. These we regard as central pillars in the horrid temple of slavery. They are both pro-slavery; and on that score, our controversy with them is based."

Douglass was not alone in his clarion call against slavery. We can't say precisely whether Philip A. Bell worked at Garrison's *Liberator* when Douglass was a stringer there, but he absorbed similar training and insight during his brief tenure at the paper. In fact, ten years after *Freedom's Journal* arrived on the scene, Bell started *The Weekly Advocate*, which Samuel Cornish edited. Later the paper was renamed the *Colored American* and was co-owned by Charles Bennett Ray, a highly respected abolitionist. At the same time Douglass was keeping readers informed in the eastern part of the country about the fight against slavery, Bell took up the struggle west of the Mississippi as the co-editor of *The Pacific Appeal*. During Reconstruction, he had his own paper, *The San Francisco Elevator*.

Any discussion of the Black press out West is incomplete without citing the conviction and courage of Charlotta Bass, who sold subscriptions at the *Eagle* before she became the owner of the paper, renaming it the *California Eagle*. She was best known for championing unpopular causes, especially as they resonated around union activity and in alliance with such leftist political figures as Paul Robeson. An unadulterated crusader, Bass was a staunch Republican and was the first African American woman to be nominated for vice president.

Often overlooked but never unappreciated was the *Christian Recorder*, which was first published in 1854. Under the editorship of Rev. J. P. Campbell, the paper, or church bulletin, was unflinching in its service to slaves who had been separated from their families and in its commitment to keeping African American soldiers abreast of the news during in the Civil War. These notices appeared on the paper's Information Wanted page. It gained its widest circulation and following when Benjamin Tanner was the editor in 1867. Tanner was the patriarch of an illustrious family, which included his son, Henry Ossawa Tanner, the great painter, and his daughter, Hallie, one of the nation's first Black female doctors. After increasing the circulation of the *Christian Recorder*, putatively the largest African American periodical in the country, Tanner, in 1884, became the editorial director of the *AME Church Review*, a resourceful publication for Black self-determination. By this time, he was Bishop Tanner.

The advent of the Civil War brought no surcease from Douglass, and by 1861, through the pages of *Douglass' Monthly*, he was just as vigorous and outspoken as ever, only now his plea to end bondage took on a religious aspect, most notably in the masthead of his paper emblazoned with Proverbs 31: "Open thy mouth, judge righteously, and plead the cause of the poor and needy." Mainly, the paper vented Douglass's central concerns, while at the same time fixing on the flow of events spilling from the war. According to one Douglass biographer, the paper "functioned like a photographic album, freezing some moments while invoking through the arrangement of stories the onward rush of the war." Even so, the *Monthly* often bristled with Douglass's critique of the state of the Union and the social and political conditions as they pertained to the "contrabands of war."

After the war, Douglass was again on the ramparts, but nevertheless continued to plead his case through the *New National Era*. "When the slave was a slave I demanded his emancipation, and when he was free, I demanded his perfect freedom—all the safeguards of freedom."

Many of those safeguards were impotent during the Reconstruction era, and the abolitionist press now had a new postbellum menace to challenge and defeat. The backlash was most terrifying in the hooded members of the Ku Klux Klan and other night riders. By the end of Reconstruction, which, other than some advances in higher education, left few benefits for Blacks who had to endure another form of slavery via peonage, the convict lease system, and outright sharecropping. A surge of lynching further endangered Black lives, particularly in the South. When three of Ida B. Wells's friends were lynched, the indomitable journalist stepped up her campaign to combat the increased attacks.

As the editor of the *Memphis Free Speech*, Wells was a fearless foe of lynching, often traveling unaccompanied to spread the word and to encourage others to take a stand. After her office was attacked by a mob, she relocated to Chicago, where her fervor against lynching found a new platform at the *New York Age*. Although she acquired some prominence from her articles in the *Age* she believed they were not reaching a wide enough audience. To expand her readership and her horizons, Wells toured Europe in 1893, lecturing on the evils of lynching. Upon her return to the states, she began working for *Conservator*, which was owned and edited by the attorney Ferdinand Barnett, whom she later married. Wells was once more in the spotlight when she and Frederick Douglass compiled a booklet to protest the 1893 World's Columbian Exposition, which barred Blacks from participating. They distributed some ten thousand copies during the fair. But it was her publication of *A Red Record*, which recounted three years of lynching, that commanded the greatest attention. Most of the data she obtained came from the *Chicago Tribune*, a white-owned newspaper, thereby protecting her from charges of bias.

The *New York Age* was founded in 1881 as the *New York Globe*, and after T. Thomas Fortune took over as editor it was even more militant in regard to the mistreatment of freedmen and women. No matter what the paper was called in its successive iterations, so long as Fortune was at the helm it was an adamant adversary of Jim Crow. The *Age* was also forthright in its support of other Black papers in the South, providing coverage of the circumstances they faced in their quest for total freedom and independence.

Other northern Black-owned papers—the *Detroit Plaindealer*, the *Philadelphia Tribune*, and the *New York Amsterdam News*—lent their voices and their resources in the battle against racism and white supremacy. Almost contemporaneously with the establishment of these pioneering norther urban papers was the *Chicago Defender*, under the leadership and guidance of Robert Sengstacke Abbott. From the paper's inception, it was ready to speak truth to power with never a moment of retreat as it waged a war against racial injustice.

Into the second decade of the 20th century, the Black press increased exponentially, and this was of special importance for the migrants from the South who traveled north looking for greater opportunities. Of course, all was not as rosy as advertised in the press; in fact, many of the hardships the new arrivals experienced in the South were evident in cities such as Chicago, Detroit, Philadelphia, and New York. Here again the Black press came to the rescue, assisting the newcomers in their adjustment to the new environment, dispensing the valuable news they needed to survive. In the same manner they had been a beacon during the terrible days of slavery, the press was there for the "blues people" who needed all the information they could get as they navigated the so-called Promised Land north of the cotton curtain.

"Between World War I and World War II, African American newspapers guided their readers through a rigidly segregated world," said narrator Joe Morton in Stanley Nelson's documentary *The Black Press: Soldiers without Swords.* "The papers provided information that was mundane but critical for African Americans' survival. Display ads suggested where they could shop without risking humiliation. Classified ads told them which employers did not discriminate. Sports and society pages lauded the athletes and professionals who the mainstream press ignored. Black newspapers showed the full spectrum of life in Black communities. In return, African American readers treated newspaper men and women with respect and adulation. In the mainstream press, Black journalists were denied the opportunity to practice their craft and earn a living, but in their world they were stars."

Those stars are strung like milestones of American history: from Russwurm to Douglass to Ida B. Wells to Sengstacke Abbott, each of them indispensable in the pursuit of liberty and justice in this nation.

Even when slavery had another name, the Black press was a reliable sentinel, an alternative to the negativity that was pervasive in the white press. And now, in these times when many Americans think we are living in a post-racial society, the Black press is here to set the record straight, and more than eager to continue to "plead our own cause."

History shows the extent to which the Black press has fought ceaselessly to beat back the racism that nowadays takes on a more venomous form of incipient fascism. In this digital age, with the advent of social media and the scourge of fake news and misinformation, the Black press is needed more than ever. And when the president of the United States can declare that journalists are the "enemies of the people," you know our predicament is worse. Actress Stacey Dash had the audacity to declare that Black History Month is no longer necessary. What she failed to understand were the conditions that made it necessary in the first place—and none of those iniquitous demons have vanished.

Similarly, the Black press is needed to combat the propaganda of right-wing or alt-right publications and media outlets that abound, packed with vicious lies and erroneous conclusions about the state of Black America. It's particularly distressing to learn that so many Americans have bought into these misconceptions, accept them without investigation and then spread them as gospel truth.

Well, we need gospel truth, not knee-jerk reactions. We need the spirit of Ida B. Wells, T. Thomas Fortune, Ethel Payne, Frederick Douglass, Hoyt Fuller, John Johnson, James Hicks, and Lerone Bennett, as well as the fearless photographers who risked their lives to capture precious moments. It was the Black press that kept us informed of the atrocities that occurred daily in our communities, tragedies that went unnoticed in the mainstream press. Our stories still need to be told, there are still far too many children suffering from contaminated water, too many incidents of domestic violence that cry out for coverage, and the law enforcement agencies from California to Maine appear to be afflicted with common rage against young Black men.

As the old-line publications disappear—or more fortunately evolve into online iterations—there is a ray of hope that they will carry on the fight for justice, carry the faith of activist journalism into the next generation.

Exemplary of this resolve is the communication from such online entities as *Black Agenda Report, The Root, The Grio, Black Press USA, Richard Prince's Journal-isms*, and the tireless work of bloggers with their columns and tweets. Several of those activist journalists have been summoned to the pages of this anthology. Yes, past is prologue, and it's time we rewind the clock to those yesteryears when the Black press was empowered, had the advertisers, the subscriptions, the intrepid reporters, visionary editors and publishers, and the moxie to plead our cause without reservations. That's the past that will give us a renewed sense of purpose, a renewed sense of possibility, and a fresh prologue of hope and promise.

For all our successes in the past, the burden of post-slavery remains, but Black people and our press are used to heavy lifting, used to rolling that Sisyphean rock off us and up the hill.

BIG MAMA'S MONEY
A LASTING LESSON FROM BONDAGE:
DON'T BE A SLAVE TO DEBT

Michelle Singletary

My financial foundation came from my grandmother, Marie Kelly, whom we called Big Mama. I inherited her hatred of debt because debt enslaves you whether it's a mortgage, student loan, or credit card. It puts you in bondage. Big Mama's grandparents were slaves. You couldn't get her to talk about it too much. It hurt too much, she said. But there's one story she told that never leaves me.

Her grandmother, who was light-skinned, was brought into the big house to nurse the slave-owner's newborn, she recounted. My great-great-grandmother was also nursing her own child. However, her left breast was supposed to be used exclusively for the white baby. And the ridiculous reason: the slave-owner's wife believed the milk from that left breast was better and sweeter because it was over the heart.

As Big Mama told it, one day her grandmother was rocking and nursing her own child. She switched breasts, as many mothers do. Perhaps the rhythm of this bond between mother and child made her forget the rule. Her child was nursing on her left breast. The slave-owner saw her and was outraged. My great-great-grandmother was beaten for making that mistake.

When Big Mama's grandparents were freed, they vowed to work hard enough to always have their own money and never be beholden to anyone. Being enslaved physically and mentally wasn't the only enslavement. Depending on those who hate you was an emotional shackle they vowed never to wear again.

That is why I come from a line of people who knew how to handle money. They were passionate savers.

My grandmother never forgot that nursing story. She used it as inspiration to handle her finances. She had only a high school education, but she never was broke. The legacy of the inhumanity of slavery led to my grandmother's determination to be a good money manager. It was also why she hated debt with a passion. She feared debt. She hated debt. She didn't like being a slave to debt.

Big Mama lived out what it says in Proverbs 22:7: "The rich rule over the poor, and the borrower is slave to the lender."

There's no qualifier in this scripture. If you are in debt, you are a slave. Having grandparents who intimately understand the horrors of slavery, my grandmother extended that to her finances.

Although my grandmother kept her cars forever, she did have car loans over the years. But she would pay them off early. One time, after she had paid off a car note, the lender called. She was told that their records showed she had missed a payment. My grandmother had paid off the loan so quickly the lender thought something was amiss.

Now, my grandmother was a praying woman. She was a Christian. But the words that came out of her mouth that day made me shake. I can only imagine how the person on the other end of the telephone line was feeling. Her anger was so unfamiliar and powerful that we cowered in a corner while she cussed out that account person.

My grandmother had two credits cards—one from Sears and one from Montgomery Ward. I'm not sure why. She rarely used them. She just saved up her cash to purchase things she wanted or needed.

Or she would put stuff on layaway. And when she did use credit, she paid off the balance before it was due.

One time Big Mama used credit to replace our washing machine, which had broken unexpectedly. With five grandchildren to care for, she couldn't go without a washer for too long, and going to a laundromat was too expensive.

Once the washer broke, we kids thought, "Oh great! Now we can get a dryer." During the winter, our fingers froze as we tried to hang laundry on the lines extending over our back porch.

"Can we get the matching dryer?" I asked.

"No, that's why God invented sunlight," my grandmother said.

Debt is evil, she would say, and as such you should use it only sparingly. We needed a washer. We could do without a dryer, especially since it meant going into debt.

Big Mama borrowed to buy a home, but she hated having a mortgage. Every time she made her monthly mortgage payment, she would pray about the day the entire debt would be gone. She lived for the moment that she could put her last mortgage payment in the mail. Shortly after she did, she retired. Once she had shed that shackle, she felt free.

Co-signing was also a no-go for her. If you asked my grandmother to co-sign a loan, it was as if you were cussing at her.

I made that mistake, just once. Out of college I needed—or wanted—a car to get to my first full-time journalism job. The dealer said I needed someone to co-sign. I asked my grandmother. She spent several hours—and I'm not kidding—lecturing me about the dangers of co-signing. I was being selfish just by asking, because it would put her finances in jeopardy, she fussed. I waited until my credit got better, and I didn't need a co-signer.

My grandmother made a believer out of me. She made me see the similarities of being a slave and being a slave to debt. Both can damage your soul.

CATCHING HANDS
AFRICAN AMERICANS AND
EVERYDAY REBELLIONS
Carolyn Edgar

I am a fighter, from a family of fighters.

That is probably why I noticed the shirt so quickly.

Shortly after the 2016 presidential election, a new T-shirt design began making the rounds on social media. The shirt, a response to the white supremacist movement empowered by the election of Donald Trump, bore varying messages along a similar theme: "Dear Racists, we are not our grandparents. Signed, These Hands."

I am a fighter—not a physical one, but an intellectual one who takes no prisoners to fight the racism that could consume me or my two young adult children. So I knew immediately what the shirt was saying: "Catch hands" is slang for a fistfight, the modern-day equivalent of "catching a beatdown" or "opening a can of whoopass on ya."

But I would never wear that shirt because it dishonors my ancestors. It implies that slaves did not fight back against a brutal apartheid that some did not survive.

It diminishes the storied resistance efforts like the civil rights movement, as Dr. Ivory Toldson and Damon Young noted in their articles about the shirts. This emphasis on honor, though well-founded, is of limited importance. What rankles about the "we are not our grandparents" meme isn't simply that it dishonors our forebears, but that it rests on the grossly inaccurate notion that people of African descent and their descendants never fought back against slavery and Jim Crow.

Dr. Henry Louis Gates, the Harvard scholar, has called the belief that slaves and their descendants were "either exceptionally 'docile' or 'content and loyal'" one of "the most pernicious allegations made against the African-American people."

Long before the civil rights movement, black people fought back against oppression, in ways big and small.

The legacy of African American rebellion may be absent from our history classes, but scholars of African American history have labored to set the record straight. The book *Runaway Slaves: Rebels on the Plantation*, by John Hope Franklin and Loren Schweninger, chronicles various acts of rebellion among slaves, from work stoppages to running away to insurrection plots. Thavolia Glymph's *Out of the House of Bondage: The Transformation of the Plantation Household* explores the struggles of freed black women to navigate shifting power dynamics in the post-Emancipation era. These struggles continued long after slavery ended, and in many ways continue today.

But one need not turn only to history books for examples of rebellion and resistance. Although my parents never marched with Dr. King and didn't refuse to sit in the back of a bus, my family legacy is rife with examples of everyday rebellion and resistance. My parents shared with us amusing—and sometimes frightening—anecdotes describing the small but significant ways that they and members of their families fought to retain their humanity and dignity while living under the Jim Crow regime that replaced slavery and sought to make them feel inferior and barely human.

My late parents were both born and raised in Jim Crow Mississippi—my father in 1921, my mother in 1930. They lived in a segregated rural community they referred to as Rock Hill. So far as I can determine, the Rock Hill community in Oktibbeha County was never formally incorporated as a separate town, and is part of the city of Starkville, home of Mississippi State University. But the Rock Hill my parents described was a world apart from Starkville, which they called "town." I have been to Rock Hill only once—for my maternal grandfather's funeral in 1972, when I was seven years old. Back then, the town looked much as my mother had described. It had not changed from the late 1940s and early 1950s—rural, hilly, and sparsely populated.

Both of my parents were raised on small farms, on land that had been owned by their families since shortly after Emancipation. Jim Crow affected their daily lives, but not in the ways commonly depicted in pop culture. Despite being owners and not sharecroppers, my parents led lives of privation and hardship, exacerbated by economic racism and inequality.

My mother, the second oldest of ten children, was raised in a two-room shack. Jim Crow denied her family routine access to medical care, with devastating effects. My maternal grandmother died of kidney failure while giving birth to her tenth child; the baby died of the same cause eighteen months later. Another of my mother's siblings died in his early twenties. A third sibling died of unknown causes as an infant.

Jim Crow denied my parents equal access to education. My parents attended underfunded and overcrowded rural schools. They received the best education available to them at the time, but, by design, it was inferior to the education provided to white children. Like many black boys who grew up in the segregated rural South during that era, my father stopped going to school after eighth grade because there were no colored high schools in Rock Hill. My mother was able to attend high school only by leaving her family in Rock Hill and moving to Starkville.

My parents left Mississippi at different points, but for the same reason—because the economic hardships that Jim Crow imposed on them became unbearable. The promise of greater fortune in the North beckoned, and they heeded the call. My father moved to Detroit with his parents when he was a teenager; my mother moved to Detroit as a young woman. They were driven out of Mississippi not by lynchings, segregated buses and lunch counters, fire hoses, or dogs, but by the brutal economic and societal impact of the Southern system of apartheid.

Yet even as racism denied my parents some of the basic necessities of life, the fact that Rock Hill was segregated from Starkville spared them the daily indignities of Jim Crow. Ironically, it also shielded them from the racist violence I once believed was a ubiquitous feature of black Southern life.

I interviewed my parents in 1992, nearly twenty years before Isabel Wilkerson's masterly tome, *The Warmth of Other Suns*, and just a few months before my father died of lung cancer. My interview was for a law school paper about the Great Migration. I had never heard the term "Great Migration" until I mentioned in passing to Randall Kennedy, my Harvard Law School professor and adviser, that I grew up in Detroit and my parents were from Mississippi.

Kennedy encouraged me to research my own family's Great Migration and compare their oral histories to the Great Migration literature. We were living examples of how black Southern culture permanently transformed Northern cities like New York; Chicago; Detroit; Gary, Ind.; Philadelphia; and St. Louis, among so many others, yet I didn't learn until I was in law school that my family's personal experience was part of a larger historical and cultural phenomenon, and that they were part of one of the largest population shifts in American history.

Armed with a few books from Kennedy's personal library and a list of many more, I went to Harvard's Widener Library to start researching.

And then my parents told me the stories the books did not.

I still remember how my father scoffed when I asked him about lynching.

"Wasn't no lynching in Rock Hill," he declared.

My mother nodded. My parents didn't agree on much, but on that they were united.

"Really?" I asked. "The books said many black people left the South to escape lynching."

"White people knew better than to come to Rock Hill," my mother said.

My parents weren't seeking to minimize the deplorable history of lynching in the South. To the contrary, my parents wanted me to know that, in the same way that black people in the South were encouraged to avoid courting trouble among white people, whites were taught not to venture alone into a rural community of black people who were armed for their own self-protection.

When I let my parents tell it, I learned that the relationship between whites and blacks in Rock Hill during the Jim Crow era was one of mutually assured destruction. You leave us alone, we'll leave you alone.

Many of the stock tropes of the Jim Crow South—whites-only water fountains and segregated buses—had no bearing on my parents' daily lives in rural Rock Hill. Blacks who worked and lived in town, from black domestic workers to middle-class blacks such as the doctors, lawyers, and undertakers that served the black community, would have dealt with segregated public facilities on a daily basis.

Poor farmers like my parents' families, however, rarely went to town unless absolutely necessary. My mother acknowledged that the movie theater in town had a colored-only section, but going to the movies was a rare enough treat that, for her, sitting in the colored section was an endurable hardship.

Poor farmers like my parents' families could limit their encounters with whites, but they couldn't avoid them entirely. The white owners of the country stores where my maternal grandfather bought his farm supplies and sold his eggs and other goods often tried to sell him merchandise for more than the listed price, and bought his goods for less than they were worth. During one such encounter, my grandfather corrected the store clerk, who apparently assumed my grandfather couldn't read—then corrected him again when the clerk tried to give my grandfather the wrong amount of change, assuming my grandfather couldn't add or subtract. There wasn't much my grandfather could do about the fact that he was paid less for his eggs and other goods than white farmers, but he insisted on getting as fair a price as he was able.

It was in Starkville, not Rock Hill, that my mother encountered the type of open, blatantly racist acts that are typically depicted in films and books about the South in the Jim Crow era. My mother had moved to town for high school—as I said, there was no colored high school in Rock Hill—and was living with her older cousin, a schoolteacher, and her cousin's daughter, who was one of the first black attorneys in town.

One night, as they were cleaning up after dinner, a group of white men—college boys from Mississippi State—drove up to my mother's cousin's house and asked if they could buy some "nigger pussy."

"Go ask your mother," replied her cousin's daughter.

This was one of my mother's favorite stories, but every time she told it, I cringed—and not only because it was disorienting to hear my mother say the words "nigger pussy." The story unnerved me because, according to lore, the car full of boys should have firebombed the house, or returned with gun-toting Klansmen, or broken down the door and raped them all. I found the story terrifying even though I knew that nothing happened—the drunk frat boys simply drove off to find what they were looking for somewhere else. The official history of Jim Crow suggested that the backtalk my mother boasted about led to certain death. There seems to be no room in the history books for a house full of black women in 1950s Mississippi telling a car full of white men to go fuck their mothers.

My parents' stories taught me that it was not only OK but absolutely necessary to speak truth to power, to stand up for what is right, to challenge the status quo, and to insist on fair treatment. Failing to talk about the everyday ways in which black people have rebelled and fought back throughout history does worse than dishonor our ancestors. It does violence to our very existence. Rebellion has not only occurred at exceptional moments in black history. Indeed, resistance is a hallmark of black existence. Every side eye is rooted in a tradition of defiance and refusal to capitulate to bondage and servitude.

I live with my parents' stories. I inherited their fighting spirit.

My son and daughter now live with their grandparents' stories, as well as their mother's stories. Because they are black, I have to teach them to have a fighting spirit, using examples from their own family's past.

For African Americans, our life's work is to teach our children the complete history of African American life in America—including our longstanding history of rebellion—to prepare our current generations to carry the burden that slavery left and to empower future generations to stand up and fight back, as our ancestors did every day.

We are still fighting back—every day.

Notes

FOREWORD

1. "... had 'clothed' Congress with 'power to pass all laws necessary. . .'" Jones v. Alfred H. Mayer Company, 392 U.S. 409 (1968). https://www.law.cornell.edu/supremecourt/text/392/409.

2. "Not everything that is faced can be changed; but nothing can be changed until it is faced." James Baldwin, "As Much Truth as One Can Bear," *The New York Times Book Review*, January 14, 1962. http://query.nytimes.com/gst/abstract.html?res=9B05E7D7153DEE32A25757C1A9679C946391D6CF&legacy=true.

INTRODUCTION

1. "Slavery was horrible, but . . ." Jack Kelly, "Remnants of Slavery," *Pittsburgh Post-Gazette*, September 13, 2015. http://www.post-gazette.com/opinion/jack-kelly/2015/09/13/Jack-Kelly-Remnants-of-slavery/stories/201509130074.

THE BURDEN

1. "Restroom break, boss?" *Shawshank Redemption*. Dir. Frank Darabont. Castle Rock Entertainment, 1994.

2. "There I was, the black grandson of a slave . . ." Jackie Robinson, *I Never Had It Made: An Autobiography of Jackie Robinson* (New York: Putnam, 1972).

3. "Well it's not an issue . . . for you." "Something Against You." *Grey's Anatomy*. ABC. November 12, 2015. https://greys228.tumblr .com/.

4. ". . . refusing to insure mortgages in and near African American neighborhoods." "A 'Forgotten History of How the U.S. Government Segregated America," *Fresh Air*, WHYY, May 3, 2017. http://www.npr .org/2017/05/03/526655831/a-forgotten-history-of-how-the-u-s -government-segregated-america.

5. ". . . assail the dignity of black schoolchildren." Emma Brown, "Judge: Mostly White Southern City May Secede from School District Despite Racial Motive," *The Washington Post*, April 27, 2017. http:// wapo.st/2vFzlN6.

6. ". . . could not prove that their actions wouldn't hinder desegregation in Jefferson County." Matthew Rozsa, "A Federal Judge Is Letting an Alabama School District Return to Segregation," *Salon*, April 28, 2017. http://www.salon.com/2017/04/28/a-federal-judge-is-letting -an-alabama-school-district-return-to-segregation/.

7. "I am not quite sure . . ." Booker T. Washington, *Up from Slavery* (New York: Doubleday, Page, 1901), 1. http://bit.ly/2ud8yZj.

8. "Rather than acknowledge that America is still dealing with the vestiges of slavery . . ." Rochelle Riley, "America's Divide Will Persist Until We Teach Children Whole History," *Detroit Free Press*, February 17, 2017. http://www.freep.com/story/news/columnists/rochelle-riley /2017/02/17/donald-trump-black-history-month/97752128/.

9. "By 1900, the South's judicial system had been wholly reconfigured. . ." Douglas Blackmon, *Slavery by Another Name: The Re-Enslavement of Black Americans from the Civil War to World War II* (New York: Doubleday, 2008), 7.

10. "The life of the Negro is still sadly crippled. . ." Martin Luther King Jr., "I Have a Dream" address delivered at the March on Washington for Jobs and Freedom, August 28, 1963. https://kinginstitute .stanford.edu/king-papers/documents/i-have-dream-address-delivered -march-washington-jobs-and-freedom.

11. "The Atlantic slave trade between the 1500s and 1800s . . ." Manny Fernandez and Christine Hauser, "Texas Mother Teaches Textbook Company a Lesson on Accuracy," *The New York Times*, October 5, 2015. https://www.nytimes.com/2015/10/06/us/publisher -promises-revisions-after-textbook-refers-to-african-slaves-as-workers .html?_r=0.

12. "Every man lives in two realms . . ." Martin Luther King Jr., "The Quest for Peace and Justice," Nobel Lecture, December 11, 1964. http://www.nobelprize.org/nobel_prizes/peace/laureates/1964/king -lecture.html.

13. ". . . as long as the Negro is the victim of the unspeakable hor-rors of police brutality . . ." Martin Luther King Jr., "I Have a Dream," address delivered at the March on Washington for Jobs and Freedom, August 28, 1963. https://kinginstitute.stanford.edu/king-papers /documents/i-have-dream-address-delivered-march-washington-jobs -and-freedom.

14. "When we do not teach . . ." Rochelle Riley, "America's Divide Will Persist Until We Teach Children Whole History," *Detroit Free Press*, February 17, 2017. http://www.freep.com/story/news/columnists /rochelle-riley/2017/02/17/donald-trump-black-history-month /97752128/.

THE ARMOR WE STILL NEED

1. "Once slaves had been . . ." Henry Wilkinson Bragdon and Sam-uel Proctor McCutchen, *History of a Free People* (New York: Macmillan, 1964), 19.

2. "Slavery was horrible, but . . ." Jack Kelly, "Remnants of Slavery," *Pittsburgh Post-Gazette*, September 13, 2015. http://www.post-gazette .com/opinion/jack-kelly/2015/09/13/Jack-Kelly-Remnants-of-slavery /stories/201509130074.

3. "The problem of the 20th century . . ." and "It is a peculiar sen-sation . . ." W. E. B. Du Bois, *The Souls of Black Folk* (Chicago: A. C. McClurg and Company, 1903), 9; 2.

A MILITARY FAMILY, DESCENDED FROM SLAVES

1. "It always appeared a most iniquitous scheme . . ." Letter from Abigail Adams to John Adams, September 22, 1774, curated by the Massachusetts Historical Society. https://www.masshist.org/digital adams/archive/doc?id=L17740922aa.

2. "He has waged cruel war . . ." From Thomas Jefferson's "original Rough draught" of the Declaration of Independence, Library of Congress. https://www.loc.gov/exhibits/declara/ruffdrft.html.

3. "In the end, the War of 1812 . . ." Gene Allen Smith, "Wedged Between Slavery and Freedom: African American Equality Deferred," National Park Service report. https://www.nps.gov/articles/wedged -between-slavery-and-freedom.htm.

REMNANTS OF SURVIVAL:
BLACK WOMEN AND LEGACIES OF DEFIANCE

1. "We should look to what happened to Korryn Gaines. . ." Wesley Lowery, "Korryn Gaines, Cradling Child and Shotgun, Is Fatally Shot by Police," *The Washington Post*, August 2, 2016. https:// www.washingtonpost.com/news/post-nation/wp/2016/08/02/korryn -gaines-is-the-ninth-black-woman-shot-and-killed-by-police-this -year/?utm_term=.7872f2d590cf; Alison Knezevich, "No Charges Filed in Korryn Gaines Shooting," *The Baltimore Sun*, September 21, 2016. http://www.baltimoresun.com/news/maryland/crime/bs-md-co -shellenberger-gaines-20160921-story.html.

LIVING WITHOUT A BEGINNING

1. "During my period of horrific self-hatred . . ." Patrice Gaines, *Moments of Grace: Meeting the Challenge to Change* (New York: Three Rivers Press, 1997), 202.

2. "self-study spiritual thought system . . ." *A Course in Miracles* (Mill Valley, Calif.: The Foundation for Inner Peace). https://acim.org /AboutACIM/.

ETERNAL BONDAGE

1. "... a black man 'had no rights which the white man was bound to respect...'" Scott v. Sandford, 60 U.S. 393 (1857). https://www.law.cornell.edu/supremecourt/text/60/393.

2. "The Nixon campaign in 1968 ..." Dan Baum, "Legalize It All: How to Win the War on Drugs," *Harper's Magazine*, April 2016. https://harpers.org/archive/2016/04/legalize-it-all/.

3. "You have to face the fact ..." H. R. Haldeman, *The Haldeman Diaries: Inside the Nixon White House* (New York: G. P. Putnam's Sons, 1994).

SPORTS INDUSTRIES AS PLANTATIONS

1. "... interpreted as a form of neocolonial exploitation...." Paul Darby, Gerard Akindes, and Matthew Kirwin, "Football Academies and the Migration of African Football Labor to Europe," *Journal of Sport and Social Issues* 31, no. 2 (2007). http://journals.sagepub.com/doi/abs/10.1177/0193723507300481.

IF AMERICA HAD BELIEVED THAT BLACK GIRLS WERE GIRLS

1. "... he said the student 'bears some responsibility' for her assault ...." Dana Ford, Greg Botelho, and Kevin Conlon, "Spring Valley High School Officer Suspended After Violent Classroom Arrest," CNN, October 27, 2015. http://www.cnn.com/2015/10/27/us/south-carolina-school-arrest-video/index.html.

2. "This is not a race issue..." Sarah Ellis, "Accountability, Race, Excessive Use of Force All Topics at the Richland 2 Board Meeting," *The State*, October 27, 2015. http://www.thestate.com/news/local/crime/article41644848.html.

3. "I'm teaching her a fucking lesson." David Boroff, "Chicago Girl, 6, Handcuffed Under Stairs at School," *New York Daily News*, August 11, 2016. http://www.nydailynews.com/news/national/chicago-girl-6-handcuffed-stairs-school-security-guard-article-1.2747642.

KALIEF BROWDER: A LIFE MARKED FOR DEATH

1. "The police system of the South . . ." W. E. B. Du Bois, *The Souls of Black Folk* (Chicago: A. C. McClurg and Company, 1903), 108.

OBJECT LESSONS:
RE-ENCOUNTERING SLAVERY THROUGH ROSE'S GIFT

1. "On that day six thousand people did not die. . . ." Rabbi Marc Gellman, prayer service at Yankee Stadium, September 23, 2001. http://transcripts.cnn.com/TRANSCRIPTS/0109/23/se.03.html.

OUR INTERNAL WAR:
EMBRACING A GREATNESS THAT SHOULD BE NORMAL

1. "Sometimes we are blessed . . ." Rudolph P. Byrd, Johnnetta Betsch Cole, and Beverly Guy-Sheftall, eds., *I Am Your Sister: Collected and Unpublished Writings of Audre Lorde* (New York: Oxford University Press, 2009), 140. http://bit.ly/2uQhwyP.

THE FOOTPRINT OF AMERICA'S RACIAL STRUGGLE IN CUBA

1. "We support Cuba's right to enjoy national sovereignty. . ." "Acting on Our Conscience: A Declaration of African American Support for the Civil Rights Struggle in Cuba," *AfroCubaWeb*, November 30, 2009. http://www.afrocubaweb.com/actingonourconscience.htm.

2. ". . . the acerbic public intellectual who once accused Barack Obama . . ." Ian Schwartz, "Cornel West on Obama: 'The First Black President Has Become The First Niggerized Black President," RealClear Politics, June 22, 2015. https://www.realclearpolitics.com /video/2015/06/22/cornel_west_on_obama_the_first_black_president _has_become_the_first_niggerized_black_president.html.

3. "A Yoruba proverb affirms . . ." Patricia Grogg, "Racial Debate Enters US-Cuba Conflict," *Havana Times*, December 6, 2009. http:// www.havanatimes.org/?p=16838.

4. "None of the governments prior to 1959 did anything for the

poor in general or for blacks in particular." Esteban Morales, "The Cuban Revolution Began in 1959," Havana Times, April 2, 2013. http://www.havanatimes.org/?p=90508,

5. ". . . the so-called internal dissidents . . ." Patricia Grogg, "CUBA: Communist Academic Recovers His Party Card," *Inter Press Service*, July 15, 2011. http://www.ipsnews.net/2011/07/cuba-communist -academic-recovers-his-party-card/.

THE WEAPON OF NARRATIVE
AND THE AFRICAN AMERICAN STORY

1. "With us, all of the white race, however high or low, rich or poor, are equal in the eye of the law." Alexander Stephens, Cornerstone speech in Savannah, Ga., March 21, 1861. https://www.ucs.louisiana .edu/~ras2777/amgov/stephens.html.

2. "History, I have often said, is a clock that people use to tell their political time of day." John Henrik Clarke, "Why Africana History?" *The Black Collegian*, 1997. http://www.hunter.cuny.edu/afprl/clarke /why-africana-history-by-dr.-john-henrik-clarke.

3. "Your ancestors dragged these black people from their homes by force . . ." Fred Jerome and Rodger Taylor, *Einstein on Race and Racism* (Piscataway, N.J.: Rutgers University Press, 2005), 86–87. http://bit .ly/2t0GWIa.

THE BLACK PRESS—MORE NEEDED THAN EVER

1. "We wish to plead our own cause." Samuel Cornish and John Russwurm, *Freedom's Journal*, 1827. http://www.indianapolisrecorder .com/opinion/article_1c0fb4b4-e958-11e6-8e63-9fe55b8c5163.html.

2. "I adopt the language of the Rev. S. E. Cornish." David Walker, *Walker's Appeal, in Four Articles* (Chapel Hill: The University of North Carolina Press, 2011), 66. http://bit.ly/2uHyCOJ.

3. "In respect to the Church and the government, we especially wish to make ourselves fully and clearly understood." Editorial, *Frederick Douglass's Paper*, June 26, 1851. In Scott C. Williamson, *The Narrative*

Life: The Moral and Religious Thought of Frederick Douglass (Macon, Ga.: Mercer University Press, 2002). http://bit.ly/2uQuyfw.

4. "... the paper 'functioned like a photographic album...'" John Stauffer, *Giants: The Parallel Lives of Frederick Douglass and Abraham Lincoln* (New York: Twelve, 2008). http://bit.ly/2tB4d0x.

5. "When the slave was a slave I demanded his emancipation...." John Stauffer, *Giants: The Parallel Lives of Frederick Douglass and Abraham Lincoln* (New York: Twelve, 2008). http://bit.ly/2vYwUpe.

6. "Between World War I and World War II, African American newspapers guided their readers ..." *The Black Press: Soldiers without Swords*. Dir. Stanley Nelson. Half Nelson Productions and California Newsreel, 1999. http://www.pbs.org/blackpress/film/fulltranscript .html.

Author Biographies

MARK AUSLANDER, PhD. is a sociocultural anthropologist, director of the Michigan State University Museum, and associate professor of anthropology and history at M.S.U. He is the former director of Central Washington University's Museum of Culture and Environment.

KEVIN B. BLACKISTONE is a panelist at ESPN, columnist at *The Washington Post*, and professor at the Philip Merrill College of Journalism at the University of Maryland.

HERB BOYD is an American journalist, educator, author, and activist. His articles appear regularly in the *New York Amsterdam News*. He teaches black studies at the City College of New York and is the author of *Baldwin's Harlem: A Biography of James Baldwin*; *Brotherman: The Odyssey of Black Men in America—An Anthology* (One World/Ballantine); and *Pound for Pound: A Biography of Sugar Ray Robinson* (Amistad, 2005).

A'LELIA BUNDLES is a biographer who writes about her great-great-grandmother Madam C. J. Walker, the early-20th-century hair care entrepreneur, and about her namesake, A'Lelia Walker (1885–1931), a central figure of the Harlem Renaissance. Bundles, a former network television news executive, has served as chair of the board of the National Archives Foundation, which supports the National Archives that houses many of America's founding and historical documents, including the U.S. Constitution and the Emancipation Proclamation.

CHARLENE A. CARRUTHERS is a black queer feminist writer, community organizer, and founding national director of the Black Youth Project 100 (BYP100). She was born and raised on the South Side of Chicago, where she lives today.

BETTY DeRAMUS is the author of two acclaimed nonfiction books: *Forbidden Fruit: Love Stories from the Underground Railroad* (2005) and *Freedom by Any Means: True Stories of Cunning and Courage on the Underground Railroad* (2009). A retired columnist for *The Detroit News*, she was formerly an editorial writer for the *Detroit Free Press* and *The Michigan Chronicle*.

CAROLYN EDGAR is an award-winning New York-based lawyer and writer whose work has appeared in *TueNight, Full Grown People, Salon,* and *The Huffington Post*. She is earning a master of fine arts degree in creative writing at the City College of New York.

PATRICE GAINES is a motivational speaker and an abolitionist who believes we must create a society that does not depend on prisons to curtail crime. She also is a writing coach and teacher, a Soros Justice Media Fellow, and author of two books, including her memoir, *Laughing in the Dark: From Colored Girl to Woman of Color, a Journey from Prison to Power*.

NIKOLE HANNAH-JONES is an award-winning investigative journalist with *The New York Times* and co-founder of the Ida B. Wells Society for Investigative Reporting, which trains investigative reporters of color. Her work has won the Peabody Award, George Polk

Award, National Magazine Award, Sigma Delta Chi Award for Public Service, and the Hechinger Grand Prize for Distinguished Education Reporting. She is writing a book on school segregation entitled *The Problem We All Live With*, to be published by the One World imprint of Penguin/Random House.

AISHA HINDS is an American television, stage, and film actress who starred as Fannie Lou Hamer in the HBO adaptation of the Tony Award-winning biographical drama *All the Way*, and was critically acclaimed for her portrayal of Harriet Tubman in WGN's historical drama *Underground*.

AKU KADOGO is a theatre director, choreographer and educator who has worked around the world. She is currently chair of the Department of Theatre and Performance at Spelman College in Atlanta, Ga.

T'KEYAH CRYSTAL KEYMÁH is an American actress, writer, singer, poet, dancer, and visual artist. An original cast member of the Fox sketch comedy series *In Living Color* (1990–94), she is perhaps best known for her roles as Erica Lucas on the CBS sitcom *Cosby* and as Tanya Baxter on the Disney Channel sitcom *That's So Raven*.

TORRANCE G. LATHAM recently completed his graduate studies at Boston University. He is pursuing one career in journalism and enjoying a second career as father to two-year-old Tamera.

PAULA WILLIAMS MADISON is an American journalist, writer, and businesswoman. She is a former NBCUniversal executive and is now partner in a Chicago-based family investment group. She produced the film *Finding Samuel Lowe*, about how nineteen Black descendants of Nell Vera Lowe Williams found and united with the three hundred descendants of her grandfather, Samuel Lowe, in China. Madison also is the author of the book *Finding Samuel Lowe* (www.findingsamuellowe.com), about the bonds among African American, African Jamaican, Hakka Chinese, and Akan/Ashanti children of the African and Chinese diasporas.

JULIANNE MALVEAUX, PhD, is an African American economist, author, social, and political commentator and businesswoman. She is president emerita of Bennett College and hosts the podcast *It's Personal With Dr. J.* She has been a contributor to *USA Today*, *Black Issues in Higher Education*, *Ms.* magazine, *Essence*, the *Progressive*, and other publications, and a commentator on CNN, BET, PBS, NBC, ABC, Fox News, MSNBC, CNBC, and C-SPAN.

TONYA M. MATTHEWS, PhD, is a spoken-word artist, president and C.E.O. of the Detroit-based Michigan Science Center, and a leader in the STEMinista movement to empower more girls to study science and engineering.

VANN R. NEWKIRK II (fivefifths) is a staff writer at *The Atlantic*, where he covers politics and policy, with a focus on voting rights, civil rights, and health policy. Vann, a co-founder of and contributing editor at *Seven Scribes*, an online magazine by young writers and artists of color, has written for *The New York Times*, *The New Yorker*, *Ebony*, *GQ* and *Grantland*, and is currently working on a science fiction novel and short story series.

LEONARD PITTS JR., whose popular *Miami Herald* column is syndicated to 250 daily newspapers, is the author of the critically acclaimed novels *Before I Forget*, *Freeman*, *Grant Park*, and the upcoming *The Last Thing You Surrender*, which will be released later this year. He is an occasional college professor, and his work also has appeared in *The New York Times*, *The Washington Post*, *Essence*, and *Reader's Digest*. He was the winner of the 2004 Pulitzer Prize for commentary.

TIM REID is an American actor, producer, director, and documentary filmmaker best known for his roles in the prime-time American television programs *WKRP in Cincinnati*, *Simon & Simon*, and *Sister, Sister*. Reid, who starred in the groundbreaking CBS series *Frank's Place* as a professor who inherits a Louisiana restaurant, is founder and president of the Legacy Media Institute, a nonprofit organization dedicated to bringing together leading professionals in the film and television industry with young men and women who wish to pursue a career in entertainment media.

ROCHELLE RILEY is an award-winning newspaper columnist who is no longer seeking permission to put the burden down. She has fearlessly called out elected officials who should have been ashamed of themselves and has helped raise millions of dollars for just causes, especially the fight for improved adult literacy. Host of her own radio talk show on 910AM Superstation in Detroit, she also makes regular appearances on MSNBC and NPR and contributes to *Essence* and *Ebony* magazines. She was inducted into the Michigan Journalism Hall of Fame in 2016, received the 2017 Ida B. Wells Award from the National Association of Black Journalists and Northwestern University in 2017 and was awarded the 2017 Eugene C. Pulliam Fellowship by the Society of Professional Journalists. She also is a global wanderer who has visited 26 countries and counting.

MICHAEL SIMANGA, PhD, is an activist cultural worker, artist and scholar in African American art and culture as expression of identity, resistance, and transformation. An instructor in the Department of African American Studies at Georgia State University, he has written, edited and published fiction, poetry, drama, essays, and memoir about the African American experience, and has produced, presented, or directed more than two hundred artistic projects including plays, exhibitions, concerts, readings, and festivals.

MICHELLE SINGLETARY is a nationally syndicated personal finance columnist at *The Washington Post* and author of *The 21-Day Financial Fast*.

DeWAYNE WICKHAM, the founding dean of the School of Global Journalism & Communication at Morgan State University, was a longtime national columnist for *USA Today* and Gannett News Service.

BENÉT J. WILSON is founder and editor in chief of Aviation Queen, LLC, an aviation and travel-writing, multimedia, and consulting business. Wilson, air travel expert for about.com and senior editor of *Airport Business* magazine, has written for *USA Today*, Airways Magazine.com, *Jetrader* and *Airport World*.

TAMARA WINFREY-HARRIS specializes in the ever-evolving space where current events, politics, and pop culture intersect with race and gender. Author of *The Sisters are Alright: Changing the Broken Narrative of Black Women in America* (Berrett-Koehler Publishers, 2015), Tamara has contributed to *The New York Times*, NPR's *Weekend Edition*, Minnesota Public Radio's *The Daily Circuit*, *Ms.* magazine, *The American Prospect*, *Salon*, *The Guardian*, *Newsweek*, *The Daily Beast*, and *The Huffington Post*.